ARCHIE NEIL

Archie Neil

From the Life *and* Stories *of*
Archie Neil Chisholm
of Margaree Forks, Cape Breton

BIOGRAPHY • ORAL HISTORY • ANTHOLOGY

by

Mary Anne Ducharme

EDITED BY RONALD CAPLAN

Breton Books
Wreck Cove, Cape Breton Island
1992

ARCHIE NEIL
From the Life and Stories of Archie Neil Chisholm
of Margaree Forks, Cape Breton

Copyright © 1992 Mary Anne Ducharme & Archie Neil Chisholm

Edited by Ronald Caplan
Production Assistance by Bonnie Thompson

ISBN 1-895415-12-8 (paperback)
ISBN 1-895415-14-4 (hardbound)

For help with the photographs, thanks to Archie Neil and Margaret
Chisholm, Priscilla Chisholm, Mary Fleck, T. Marie Chisholm.
Darkroom work: Vaughan Merchant and Carol Kennedy.

Editor's Note: In an attempt to keep alive the sound, story, and power of
Archie Neil's life, this book is a combination of biography, oral history,
and stories. It is written with the same restrictions and freedoms as an his-
torical novel. While both real and fictional names are used, *Archie Neil* is
solely the biography of Archie Neil Chisholm.

Canadian Cataloguing in Publication Data
Ducharme, Mary Anne, 1943-
    Archie Neil
ISBN 1-895415-12-8 (pbk.) — ISBN 1-895415-14-4 (bound)
1. Chisholm, Archie Neil. 2. Storytellers — Nova Scotia — Margaree
Forks — Biography.
3. Folklore — Nova Scotia — Cape Breton Island.
I. Chisholm, Archie Neil. II. Caplan, Ronald.
III. Title.
GR113.5.C36D82   398.2'09716'9   C92-098615-3

Breton Books
Wreck Cove
Cape Breton Island
Nova Scotia
B0C 1H0

CATALOGUE AVAILABLE

In a letter to Archie Neil Chisholm,
his son, R. L. Chisholm, wrote,

"Ne'er my past be gone—
E'er my past be my future"

•

Contents *of* Archie Neil

This is Archie Neil speaking:

This book has been based on true incidents from my life. Most of the names are fictitious. For instance, there never was a Nora. I'm too much of a gentleman to heap my early life on the shoulders of people with real names. Conversations have been added to scenes, but in an essential way, every single incident is true.

The lady who wrote this account of my life, Mary Anne Ducharme, has meant a great deal to me these past few years. One of the first times I met her was at a sort of literary conclave, readings of stories and poetry, at a festival in Marble Mountain. I had been approached by other people to write a biography, but I felt it would be too difficult. But I liked what I heard that day when Mary Anne was reading one of her stories. She eventually persuaded me that my life story was worth telling. She has helped me see that I had reasons for pride despite the errors of my life and the struggles that resulted from them.

The other person who put my life story in print is Ron Caplan, the editor of *Cape Breton's Magazine*. A few years ago, he visited me, and I related some of the stories of my life, and misbehaviours. He also helped me relive past struggles, and gain from them a sense of accomplishment and self-respect.

Late in my life, when I felt I hadn't any more to offer the world, people like Mary Anne Ducharme and Ron Caplan came along. This book is a way to give others a sense of what my life meant in this world.

I was born on May 25, 1907, but my first clear memory was when I had polio at the age of four. It was different then for polio victims, much harder. Our local horse doctor knew as much about it as any medical man. It was a time when the handicapped were kept at home in back rooms or attics. A lot of people thought that I was "tetched" in mind as much as I was crippled in body. I know what it is like to be the prisoner of a handicap.

The odds were against me in many ways. When I was young, handicapped people did not get jobs or education, and unemployment for the handicapped approached 98%. I was lucky, because I was given the chance to teach. There are physical impossibilities that a handicapped person must accept. But even in jobs within the capability of a crippled person, there was a time when you need not apply.

Despite all that, there was enjoyment too in my childhood. Momma beguiled my hours at home with Gaelic songs; and she truly relished telling a good story. Fiddle music and kitchen rackets were part of the life of the Forks when I was young. My father, known as "Archie the Teacher," taught me at home, and was a man of wit and humour. I fought with and played pranks on my eight brothers and sisters.

I knew what it felt like to be laughed at by my peers because I was crippled. But I could stand that better than pity. Anyone who said something like "Poor Archie Neil, isn't it too bad he had to be like that"—that would put me in a blazing rage. This feeling has never left me, even now in my 85th year. I might not say anything, but my thoughts could blister paint. An old politician had a neighbour who hated him and wrote him an abusive letter. The politician did not want to respond in kind. So he asked his secretary to type out an answer. The letter said: "Dear Sir, My Secretary, being a lady, I cannot have her write down the things that I think you are. I, being a gentleman, would not say them anyway. But you, being neither, will understand what I mean."

In looking at the long perspective about polio in my life, I think it helped me to understand a lot more about humanity than I otherwise would have. I have found kindness where I least expected it; I have found charity in the form of love and giving. I have been helped by total strangers. That help has taken many forms, from the gift of a cup of coffee in an airport, to the gift of a little wagon when I was eight. These are experiences I would not have missed for the world.

I want to tell you the story of that wagon because it meant so much to me then, and it still does. At eight, I was able to read books to occupy myself, but I was alone and restless, and time was very long. Allan James MacInnis and his brother John Duncan were older; they lived the full active life of healthy boys and had no particular reason to think about me at all.

One day I crawled up a low hill in the back of our house— just to sit there and look around. I heard a squeaking noise on the road, and saw Allan and Duncan coming up the road over the dust and gravel and pebbles, and they were hauling a little wagon. I didn't know what it was. They swung into the lane of our house and showed me the wagon they had made. I thought it was the nicest thing I had ever seen. It had four wheels which were slices of log with auger holes for the two axles. There were no cotter pins or washers, but the boys drove large nails at the end to hold the wheels in place. They nailed a long board between the tow axles for a seat. In the centre of the front axle, they attached a bolt, with a rope to the right and left side of the axle so you could steer the wagon.

I thought they had just brought it to show me. But no, they took me up the hill and one of them coasted down, showing me how to sit and steer. I was thrilled. I wished they would stay forever with their wagon. They were on their way home and seemed to be forgetting it. I called them to come back and get it, but they turned around and said, "No, we made it for you."

There are many things I would change about my life if I could, but nothing takes precedence over my pride in being a teacher. Maybe part of it was loving an audience. Nothing made me happier than getting students to love reading. Former students still come up to me, themselves white-haired; they remember the stories and poetry I taught them. When I give a talk to senior citizen groups, I find many of my old students among them, and I still call them "boys and girls." They get a great charge out of that and so do I. I used humour in the classroom to get the students to laugh. Once they laugh, they are yours.

Humour is a great tool in many circumstances, and we need a lot more of it in this world. I remember one student who just wasn't doing anything. He was withdrawn and never participated and other teachers gave up on him. Then one day, we were studying figures of speech. As an example, I said that a girl was so skinny that if she drank tomato juice you could use her for a thermometer. It hit his funnybone. He burst out laughing, right out loud, and I had never so much as heard his voice before in class. So I went to work and kept him laughing. That seemed to change his attitude.

People thought that I was happy-go-lucky, thoughtless, because I loved a joke and a good time. But now and then what I really felt got away from me, and that was when I drank. People use many excuses for alcoholism, and mine was being crippled.

My parents tried to tell me, my true friends tried to tell me about the mistakes I was making, but I wouldn't listen. So I had to pay the price, a price nobody will ever fully know.

During my middle years, the wheels were turning, life was moving on, and I realized my opportunities were slipping away. The greatest bitterness of all was that I could not fool myself.

I had a double handicap: one physical, and the one I created for myself. I accept the blame as being the author of my own personal misery, but society provided temptation everywhere. It was part of the bounty paid for your entertainment and music ability—hours and hours of music. For that you got a thank you, a "you're a hell of a good fellow," a slap on the back, and a lot of drinks. That wasn't the case only with me, but with many fiddlers, and it cost them dearly.

Today, thank God, most of the young fiddlers I know are completely free of this curse, and they appreciate their own talents.

It is likely that every person who reads this book knows an alcoholic. We all know of careers ruined, talents wasted, families torn apart, mental and physical health destroyed. If I could prevent one more tragedy, then all the risk I have taken in revealing my alcoholism in this book, and all the hours of effort, are worthwhile. I could have made things easy by hiding the dark side, and dwelling on the humour and fun, but this would not be me, and not the whole truth. I am too close to infinity for hypocrisy at this stage of my life.

In 1950, when I quit drinking, I had a lot of catching up to do in my life. Since that time, when I was able to help another person with a drinking problem, or any problem, I felt that a little of the self-created misery in my past life was erased. I have spoken to many Alcoholics Anonymous groups, a lot of people who have given up on themselves, and I know it is useless to preach. So I make them laugh at me, at the stupid things I did, like the time I was almost arrested while riding in a wheelbarrow. That makes them take notice because they think this man is a load of crock. But by the end, they are laughing, not only at me but at themselves, because they recognize themselves in it too. A good laugh does more than preaching any day of the week.

It was only in my later life that I truly began to live. This is largely due to my wife, Margaret, who married me despite the warnings of many people. They told her, "You're taking an awful risk: he's handicapped, and an alcoholic, and you don't know when he'll fall off the keg again." She was 29 and I was 47, but I think she knew me better than I knew myself. She took the chance. Her life with me has not been an easy one. Only four months after we were married, my physical handicap was made far worse by a fall. Gradually, I lost mobility, and now am confined to a wheelchair. We have never been wealthy and we have gone through a lot of hardships together, but it was always together.

Besides mothering our children and her housekeeping, Margaret worked at any job she could get to keep our family going financially. In the years when I could no longer drive, she got me where I wanted to go at great expense to her own personal time. I am sometimes stubborn and I have been known to lose my temper. But she let me know when I was wrong-headed about things. Nowhere in this world or the next is there a better wife than Margaret has been for me.

I worked, and Margaret with me, with every charitable organization that I was ever asked to work with, some of them for four decades. I still work for them. It is part of an inner drive that I can't seem to help; maybe it is part of the struggle to repair any damage I have done to anybody in my alcoholic years. It is hard to understand the force that drives. People ask me why I keep going at my age, and they tell me I should relax and let somebody else do the things I have been doing for so long. The answer is simple: if I were compelled to desist in my work, and in association with society, I would not care to live.

My family will not have to hang their heads because I did not leave a positive mark in my passing.

When life begins, you are helpless and dependent upon others. Unless you are lucky, you end your life helpless and dependent upon others. Now I am almost back to the days when I had to face life crawling. I am ending my life confined to a wheelchair. It comes around as a circle.

What would I do if I had to live my life over again? I am tempted to say that I would not want to live my life over again, especially the first 43 years, but I know that is not true. Probably the word that sums up my life is "struggle." But I had fun too, and there are many memories that still make me laugh.

Archie Neil

PART ONE

CHAPTER 1

"Momma!" Archie Neil wailed as from a deep black well, at the bottom of which was terror, and at the top of which was a funnel of dim light that was early dawn. In the familiar place of light, his bed was horribly clutching him.

It was pulling him hard by the neck—his head touched his back and he couldn't move it. His body was a fiery, tearing ache.

Angus was still asleep next to him, one chubby arm flung over him, but Angus wasn't pulling Archie Neil's head back. Someone was crying, and it came to Archie Neil that it was himself. Crying louder, desperate, until it seemed to him that all there was to him was that sound. "Momma!" Angus sat up and looked at him, then started to wail.

Momma came first, in her nightgown, took him up in the dark. She felt his head wrenched back. She screamed, "Archie!" her strong body trembling. Her panic brought her husband from the entry shed; he had just come from the barn.

Papa scrambled up the stairs into the room, found the kerosene lamp and lit it. The older children crowded in behind him. Angus was still screaming, standing on the mattress, hopeless. Papa thought something was wrong with Angus and scooped him up, and then put him down fast when he saw the twisted body in his wife's arms. "For God's sake, Belle."

"Archie, get help."

Angus ran to Willena, whimpering, and clung to her. Momma and Papa were frightening all of them. Archie Neil tried to move his head, but something held it like iron, and Momma's tight grasp made him cry out more.

"What is wrong with him, Belle?"

"Cha'n eil fios agam! Tha am fiabhras air!" Momma's voice was harsh, speaking Gaelic. "I don't know! The fever is on him!" She put him down on the bed, and then snatched him up again, afraid to let him out of her arms. "Momma's here, Archie Neil," she kept saying, "Momma's here, don't be afraid. Na biodh eagal ort. You'll be all right. You be a good boy, now." Her hair covered him like a veil, her familiar scent began to comfort him.

"Jack," Papa ordered the oldest boy, "get the horse. Quick! Go to MacDonald's. Isabel's still visiting there. She's a trained nurse. Go!"

He forced Belle to put the four-year-old in his own arms, then gently set the twisted body down on the bed and removed the nightshirt. Archie Neil's body was hot, his back and neck rigid—his head still rammed back.

"The rest of you get out of here! All of you. Willena, take Angus out—we don't know what this is."

Archie Neil hated the touch of the sheets. He wanted to go to the brook where he and Angus played yesterday; in his mind, he saw it dappled with patches of brilliant amber light and shade—and he jumped in, and Angus was there with him, splashing, sturdy tanned bodies having fun.

Then he remembered that yesterday Grandfather MacLennan visited, a very old man with a white beard. Archie Neil was racketing about the house with Angus, rowdier than his mother approved, and she'd caught him up with a swoop of one long arm and whacked him on the bottom and made him sit in a chair quietly for ten mortally long minutes. Grandfather laughed at him, tweaked his ear hard, and told him in Gaelic that he was a big, light-headed imp.

Then in the torrid kitchen, Grandfather and all the children ate fresh cod and new potatoes and garden peas and thick, creamy milk cooled in its can in a shaded, deeper part of the brook. Then Archie Neil and Angus went out again to play while Momma cleaned the kitchen and washed dishes with Willena. It was so hot. He was consumed with thirst.

He wanted to float in the cool water of the brook, but it was not deep enough, so he decided to make a boat out of a stick, balancing a broad leaf of sail on one end, carefully placing a beetle on board and wanting to be a beetle floating on a leaf. He and Angus created waves that sent the boat rocking and spiralling until the stick, leaf and beetle parted and floated separately down the brook. Then the brothers splashed at each other, and their high-pitched yells and laughter were getting farther away, floating, and Archie Neil was in the sound, going over the tops of the trees, onto the roof of the barn, over the house and over all the people on the road to Margaree Forks, over the river to the end of the world where he had not yet been.

He could see all this far below him and he listened to his laughter as if it belonged to somebody else. Then the puppy, Snap, galloped round and around the boys, in and out of the water, and Archie Neil could hear Momma calling him to come home and he wanted to come back and play with Angus and Snap in the brook.

"I cannot be sure, Mrs. Chisholm, but I think it is spinal meningitis." It was Isabel MacDonald's voice. "Send for Dr. MacNeil at the Harbour."

Later, a man's voice told them, "Pack him in ice. I think Isabel is right about the meningitis, but there may be something else.... For God's sake, watch his breathing, don't leave him alone for a moment."

"We'll take him to the hospital in Sydney," Papa decided, turning at once to the hall stairs. The doctor moved to block his way, and Papa assured him, "We can take ice with us."

"There's nothing they can do in Sydney. The boy is too sick for a trip like that. Archie, it's too far. He's better off here."

Papa wanted to argue but Momma told him to get the ice. "The hotel, Dougald Campbell's."

A long time later, Archie Neil was floating, he was not in the brook. He was in the Margaree River where it was broad and deep, and very, very cold, so that he shivered and burned. He saw himself and Angus clad only in the old bloomer pants that once belonged to their older brothers, and they were playing by the bank and he looked down at his sturdy, chunky legs refract-

3

ed in the water, at the spread of strong toes on the smooth stones—and suddenly he felt as if he had slipped under, was drowning, he could see his own face just under the surface, and he strained upwards but his legs did not obey him. He became so tired. Very tired. And he gave in to a troubled sleep.

"Momma!" he called out upon awakening, for his body had not been released from the vice. Momma rubbed him gently with coconut butter. He did not think she was afraid now. She bathed him with cool water and sang Gaelic songs, and he fell back asleep in her arms.

In this way, days and nights blurred together with Momma or Papa always there when he woke up, and he was now in a bed in their room off the kitchen, and the vice that twisted his neck and back had eased a little, the fire raged less, but the tearing pains in his legs remained.

One day Momma caught herself at the top of the stairs, thinking of the pig they had not wanted to sell, and of old Mrs. McKeigan wanting that pig—and that the old woman might have put her eye on our pig. Or she could have given Archie Neil the Evil Eye. And for just an instant Momma wanted to go as she had seen her own father go when the horse was down, sick—go to a brook and take water with dishpan, put a coin in that water and pray over it, and then slash Archie Neil's body with the silver water from one end to another, just as her father had slashed water over the horse. She steeled herself against believing it. It isn't the Evil Eye, she told herself. It isn't the Evil Eye. This is God's. Mrs. McKeigan surely had not gone through the Margarees cutting down children with a covetous eye. Momma would not accept this. She would not. Although she could see her father coming back from the horse, the dishpan turned upside down and the silver coin now stuck solid to the bottom of the pan. And perhaps an hour later that horse was up, well, eating its way along tall grass at the side of the barn.

This is not the Evil Eye, she told herself, starting down the steps. This is not the Evil Eye. But why would God?

One day Archie Neil awoke, the room in sunlight. He could hear his brothers playing outside, the brisk crackle of fire in the

kitchen stove, the movements of someone in the kitchen, perhaps Willena, perhaps Momma—all common sounds. They
were not the nightmares. Lingering, however, was the image of
a black horse. He was alone in the bedroom, content to listen in
a heavy numb calm. There was another noise, something going
by on the road—the creaking of wagons and carriages, and the
measured crunch of hooves.

"What is it, Momma?" Archie Neil asked. "Is it the black
horse?"

Something dropped in the other room and Momma came in
quickly. She looked startled.

"What black horse?" she asked, touching his cheek, surprised to find it cool.

"I don't know," he said, losing the image that a moment before had been clear. "What is it?"

"It's Johnnie Myles McDaniel's funeral going by," she
said. "Johnnie died. You remember the pretty cemetery at
North East Margaree. Well, that's where they are going."

She picked him up and carried him into the kitchen. The
black-draped pine casket passed the window. It was on boards
in the back of an express wagon, and Archie Neil was impressed by the driver who sat up straight and solemn. He recognized the black horse.

"When will I go there?"

Momma did not answer.

On another day, he turned to see if Momma was sitting by his
bed, and he was surprised that he could move his head easily.
The headache was duller now. He felt better. Momma was
there, wrapped in her shawl, exhausted, her face smudged with
dark circles under her closed eyes, her head rested awkwardly
against her hand, asleep. He was thirsty. On a table across the
room was a pitcher of water, and he said softly, "Tha am pa-
thadh orm," but Momma did not stir. He felt reluctant to wake
her. He decided to get his own water. He shoved his legs to the
edge of the bed and then pulled on fists full of sheet until he was
able to slip over the edge, his feet falling and touching the floor.
He tried to stand and walk. There was nothing to hold him, as if
his legs did not belong to him. He could feel pain in them, but

5

they did not obey him. He let go of the sheet and thumped down hard on the floor, waking his mother with his wail.

"I was afraid of this," Dr. MacNeil said, settling the sapped child into bed after several attempts to help him stand or even maintain a sitting position. Archie Neil was now a sack of bone and flesh, his colour was sallow, but the doctor assured everyone that he was no longer in danger. "There is little function in his right leg, and practically none in his left. His lower back isn't much use to him either. It could have been worse, you know. If it had got his lungs."

Papa sucked in a deep breath. "Then what is this?"

"Infantile paralysis."

"What does that mean?"

"It means he can't walk."

"How do you cure it?"

"No cure, Archie. Maybe he will outgrow it."

Belle folded her arms across her chest against some deep ache, but her voice was calm and resolute.

"There must be something we can do." She looked toward Archie for something. "There has to be—"

"Belle, I'm sorry," Dr. MacNeil interrupted sharply. Then after looking out the window for a moment, he said more carefully, "Nobody knows. Try camphorated ointment to relieve the discomfort. Massage with cocoa butter and work his legs to keep circulation. To keep muscles from wasting away. That's all."

He took his medical bag from the chair and gave her a round metal tin of ointment, then viciously closed the bag. "Look, I have to go. Maurice Dunn has it too, but not so bad. And Billy Tompkins, over at Emerald—in his spine. I don't know how much damage has been done. I'll be back when I can." He hurried out of the room.

"Then it is catching?" Belle asked, following him. She had asked this same question a dozen times before.

"I don't know," he said, pausing at the door. "Did Maurice visit here?"

"No, he never did."

"Then they did not catch it from each other. Look, I just don't know. I think he is past the infectious stage. So far there's no sign in your other children. But keep them all away from Archie Neil, for now. In case."

"What's wrong with him?" Angus whispered again to Danny and Danny was just tired of it. They slept together now. They spoke to each other in a blend of Gaelic and English. To Momma they spoke Gaelic, to Papa English. Because Papa was a schoolteacher.

They were often awakened by crying downstairs and the sound of Papa pacing the floor, and the smell of his pipe. Momma's patient voice drifted up to them, then her quiet singing, and they knew that she was trying to get Archie Neil back to sleep. Danny was six and Angus thought that he ought to know more than he did. He was full of anxiety.

"I don't know," Danny said with a shrug. "He's sick. Tha e tinn."

"C' uige? Why?"

"I don't know," Danny said, after a pause in which their brother wailed downstairs.

"Is he going to die?" asked Angus.

"No. Only old people die."

"Boys never die?"

"No."

"But Calum drownded in the river, summertime. I heard Papa tell Momma."

"He drownded. Archie Neil is only sick."

They lapsed into silence, neither one very sure that boys didn't die.

CHAPTER 2

Now Archie Neil didn't cry so much at night. He must be better, and Angus and Danny could not understand why Momma still wouldn't let him out of bed to play. They did not like being in bed for a minute more than they had to be.

They stood in the doorway, wearing their coats, watching for Momma. She was at the scrub board in the kitchen. The other children were at school, and Angus and Danny wandered around, peeking into Archie Neil's bedroom when Momma was not watching, waiting.

When she went outside to hang the laundry in the November sun, they went right into the room and stood studying Archie Neil. They had been together nearly every day of their lives. They looked at him, and looked for the thing that had come between them.

Danny clutched Archie Neil's coat in his arms. He had wrestled it off of the high hook in the entry shed.

"Come out and play," Danny said. "Big pile o' leafs down."

"Momma's out back," Angus informed him. "She won't see us. Put on your coat, and we'll go."

"No," Archie Neil said. His refusal felt to him like some obscure obstinacy that he ought to just give up.

"How come?"

"Chan eil!" Archie Neil repeated, louder. He pursed his lips and scowled at something in mid-air that annoyed him beyond words. Then suddenly: "All right," he decided. "I'll go."

9

He tugged himself onto his side by clutching at the sheets, pushed the hateful bedding away from his legs. Biting his lip in the effort, he moved his right leg slightly, but the left one refused to follow. Rolling to his stomach, he grasped a rung of the iron bedstead and tried to pull himself up, but there was no strength in his arms, his whole body was trembling and taut, the veins in his arms and face bulging. It hurt him, but he kept pulling at the dead weight of his lower body.

His brothers made a move to help him, which was met with a look of such fury that they stepped right back. The coat slipped from Danny's hands and fell in a heap on the floor.

Archie Neil reached to his bedside table and furiously hurled a glass of water at them. It missed and broke on the wooden floor.

"Go away!"

At this Angus and Danny just stood there.

"I'll tell Momma!" Angus said, nervous.

"I'll tell Momma you did it." Archie Neil made his tone as hateful as he could. "Put my coat back!"

Danny got the broom and cleaned up the glass. Then he disappeared out the front door with the dustpan, going to a place near the barn where he and Angus hid anything they broke. Angus stayed at the doorway, he dared not go back in. When Danny came back for the coat, Archie Neil was turned to the wall, the blanket drinking hot tears.

Days passed. Archie Neil listened to children laughing in the snow. He relished the errant drafts of the cold air that came in with them to the kitchen, and he could smell the chill metal of their skates and damp wool socks when they came back from skating on the river. He listened while other children joined them coasting down the hill in back of the house, or down the hill at Peter Pat Coady's.

Yes, this obstinacy of his about not playing was a firm one, and he nursed it along in the constant ache of his legs. On some days he bawled because of the ache, making himself and his mother even more miserable; but in the end he had to stand it, had to live with it.

Archie Neil became an acute observer of sounds and smells. He knew where everyone was in the house, and could detect with great accuracy who was visiting. He knew them by whether they smelled most of cows or sheep or horse, or by the smoke of their pipes or cigars. He knew women's perfumes, the way they spoke or laughed. They often brought food and enquired about "the poor dear." He strained to hear them. He suspected Momma and Papa had secrets about him, that possibly he was going to die.

Archie Neil knew who was out of bed at night, and the next day sometimes told Momma. One day he told his sister Mary Ann that he would tell Momma that she had not changed her underwear in over a week. She told him that he was a stinking liar. He told her that he knew the drag on her bureau drawer. It hadn't been opened in a whole week. After that, Mary Ann pulled the drawer open anytime she was in the room, just to leave no doubt.

Most visitors to the Chisholm home kept their distance from Archie Neil, even if he was sitting on Momma's lap. Except Great-Aunt Lizzy, with her pug of grey hair and her clubby shoes and the two canes she needed to walk. Great-Aunt Lizzy frightened him. She called him her Gille Bochd and drenched him in wet kisses. She would recommend old cures and tonics, some of which Momma tried, and Archie Neil suffered the gas. And she would tell stories about Tom Crubach, Crippled Tom, "who was no more good to himself than a sack of beans." Tom Crubach was taken outside now and then in a wheelbarrow for an airing, and to see the sights.

Archie Neil liked it better when he had Momma alone.

There were pleasant days, when Momma had time to rock him for an hour in the afternoon, singing "ceòl-beòil," a humming mouth music, simple musical rhythms and melodies that soothed him, coming like the pulse in her breast against his cheek. She sang when she laid him on the bed and worked his bony legs, or held his arms and drew him up into a sitting position, then lowered him down in rhythm. He loved when she sang about the brown-haired maiden, holding him and rocking the chair to "Ho ro hugorin o ho / Ho ro hugorin o ho / Ho ro hugorin o / Hugorin o ro bha." She told him the story that went

11

with the song about the great mountains, "O chì, chì mi na mórbheanna / O chì, chì mi na corrbheanna / O chì, chì mi na coireachan / Chì mi na sgoran fo cheò." Or if he was restless, it was the March of the Cameron Clan, all about bagpipes over moorland and glen and light footsteps, "the March of the Cameron Men! It is the March!... It is the March! The March of the Cameron Men!" He could almost hear them coming, his own legs marching in air, his tiny ankles in his mother's hands.

She told him that there had been many bards among her MacLennans, generations back to the Kintail MacLennans in the Highlands of Scotland. And she sang songs she had learned from Archie's people, the Strathglas Chisholms. She sang about drownings of good men, cast up on the beaches among the sea wrack; she sang the Johnnie Doyle Ballad: "There's more trouble in my mind than poor tongue can e'er express." He listened closely to the song of Grey Donald's Daughter, of the woman who lured her sister to drown among the dulse on the rocky shore, her brown hair floating on top of the sea and her silver broach found on a rock. Momma sang of mountain dales, of heather-hollows, valleys of kindness, and red moss growing over cold hearths from which her people were driven. When he listened to Momma sing, everything else was forgotten.

But there were many days when Momma could not help him. Sometimes he bumped his head or a hand against the bedstead for hours in his own hypnotic rhythm. Still, he was beginning to realize that the amount of pain he had became balanced with what he could stand. He was getting stronger now, and consumed with restlessness.

He would haul himself up in bed, raised on the flat of his hands, and from his window he could see the soft April green on the gnarled limbs of the elm, limbs which all winter had rattled naked, as if also in pain. He saw the grass in the yard, pressed and dunny brown from the weight of snow, now beginning to be laced with gold-green near the south side of the house. Papa told him that dripping icicles meant that the Margaree River would soon break through its manacle of ice, perhaps even flood before the ice cleared.

Last spring Papa took him down to the river to watch the ice cracking, thrusting up in jumbled piles with mud and river grass

12

clenched in its underside, then swept into the torrents of black-water. Now inside, he recognized the fresh earth smells that found him through the door or a window or on a visitor's clothes.

The advent of spring told him again that he was trapped. Angus came in the house breathless with news that a calf was being "borned" and everyone went right out to the barn, and Archie Neil was forgotten. He sat in bed and cried. At last Jack remembered and came back in, gathered him up in the blankets and carried him to the barn. Archie Neil hugged him with grati-tude. He saw the brown-and-white calf twitching and steamy-slimy-wet, taking its first breath. It strained its neck upward, shaking its ears, then folded its front legs under, heaved up onto its wavering stilts only to be tumbled by the cow who snuffed at her baby and licked him. They all laughed, and the calf struggled up again, seeking the warm udder.

Archie Neil caught a glimpse of Mary Ann as she passed his door, her hair wound up on a towel. He knew that she was about to sit by the kitchen stove to brush it dry. He could hear Momma with her in the kitchen, kneading bread dough. He had already looked a hundred times at the patterns of waterstains on the ceiling, tracing with his finger the shape of a big A, an E, a C, a B. He found these letters in the tattered R.T. Holman's cat-alogue. When Papa was home, he helped him sound out the let-ters, and in the catalogue he picked at the riddle of the words under the pictures, the way he picked at loose threads in his woven coverlet until he had pulled them free. He was tired of looking at letters today.

"Mary Ann," he yelled, "I want something to eat." It was not time for a meal, and he was not hungry, but it was something to do, and she would not dare to refuse him in front of Momma.

"I'm busy," Mary Ann answered. "Do it yourself." There had been skirmishes between them all week. She was the feisti-est of the sisters, the least inclined to tolerate his tyranny. This posed an interesting challenge.

"Maw-ma," he bawled out, "Mary Ann won't bring me anything to eat!"

Momma told Mary Ann that it wouldn't hurt her to warm up leftovers. "Now hop to it, my girl."

"I won't," she said. "He just ate an hour ago. All he does is yell for this, yell for that. Half the time he doesn't even want it. I'm sick of him!"

Momma said, "There is corned beef in the dish."

Mary Ann dumped the meat into a huge pan, mashed cold boiled potatoes into it, banged it onto the stove. While it heated, she kept her wrath warm by brushing her hair with vengeance. When the mess in the pan had scorched black on the bottom, she scraped it into the bowl and carried it to Archie Neil with a big serving spoon thrust into the top like a flag. She filled the spoon with an enormous bite and poked it at him.

"Eat!" she insisted. "Eat it all! I hope you get a bellyache."

Whereupon Archie Neil swept his arm, hitting the bowl, the food splattering in steamy gobs on the bedding and floor.

"Momma!" he bellowed.

When Momma came to the door, the set of her face did not bode well for either of them; but after a quick assessment, she said, "Mary Ann, you clean this up!"

"I didn't spill it. He dumped it. Let him clean it up."

Momma made a slight movement towards the mutinous girl, inspiring a little prudence, and she said, "Yes, Momma!"

"Serves you right," Momma said to Mary Ann. "I told you not to tease him."

Mary Ann marched off for a rag.

Papa sat with his chair tipped against the wall near Archie Neil's bed, dressed in the fine clothes he wore when he taught school. Archie Neil watched his father, admired him. Papa drew on the curved briar pipe, studying the rising smoke. The *Casket* newspaper was on his lap; he had been reading aloud and then helping Archie Neil sound out the headlines. Most of the stories were about the sinking of a ship called the *Titanic*. It had happened in some place that was not Cape Breton but bodies from the disaster were brought to the island. Archie Neil envisioned the sinking in terms of Momma's songs of shipwrecks and of drownings at sea.

Papa was away teaching during the week, and now Archie Neil basked in his attention. He traced out the headlines with his finger and he tried very hard to say what the stick lines said.

On this Friday evening it was raining, and Papa spent a leisurely hour with his son. But there was something on his mind.

Finally, Papa stopped studying his own pipe smoke and spoke to Archie Neil as he always talked to children, as if they were reasonable adults.

"Kind of dull in here all day, Archie Neil." This wasn't a question. "I'd be good and sick of these walls by now. What do you think about eating with the rest of us, starting tomorrow?"

"Yah, Papa. I want to feed myself."

"Of course you do. But there's trouble with sitting."

"I fall down. Off the chair."

"Well, you and me, we'll fix up something tomorrow so you won't fall off. Now, let me see your arms. Make a muscle."

Archie Neil showed him his scrawny arms.

"You could use more muscle, don't you think?"

"Yah. Momma moves me."

"Well," Papa said, "tomorrow we are going to start some harder exercises, too."

The next day, using lengths of harness, Archie Neil and Papa experimented, propping him with pillows and strapping him in a straight wooden chair. Archie Neil relished the vertical view of the world. He could survey countertops and tabletops, and look at people from angles that did not emphasize chins and nostrils. And he did not have to be fed.

Despite the cushions and pillows, it was not long before his lower back cramped, and he became desperate. At last, strained and trembling, in dire need to be out of the chair, he said, "Papa, I can't."

Papa loosened the straps and took him on his lap, but after the chair even that was unbearable.

"Put me on the floor," he asked, not wanting to be a crybaby in front of Papa, if he could help it.

"It's just the first day," Momma said. Archie Neil's face was white. "We'll try again tomorrow, Papa, a little while every day."

Momma brought in a small hooked rug from the parlour. It did little to make the floor soft, and nothing to make it less drafty, but Archie Neil wanted to be where people were.

There were crumbs under the table that he could identify from the day before, and dust kittens Willena had missed. Snap, now a large dog, took liberties licking his face, or lying down next to him, huffing. He fended off the dog with a determined fist that rarely hit a satisfying mark, and Snap scarcely took notice. Worse, Mary Ann wore old shoes crushed down at the heel and she enjoyed flapping them on the floor when she walked by him.

Roddy took off his shoes when he came in from the barn, and deliberately sat close to Archie Neil, his socks a few inches from his nose.

"Roddy, your feet stink."

Everyone in the upperworld laughed, but to the underworld, it was not funny.

On the floor in the parlour, Papa would often rub and flex Archie Neil's limbs, making Archie Neil push against him with the right leg which had a little strength, and then with the left leg which had almost none. He encouraged Archie Neil to use his stomach muscles to fold the useless legs under him, get into a crawling position, and to raise his upper body on his arms. He gave Archie Neil things to lift and pull against, building his arms and shoulders.

Archie Neil fought with the dead weight of his lower body. He tried to join sides with Papa in a battle fought between Papa's will and Archie Neil's muscles that did not obey, that resisted and punished him viciously, and did not care what Papa wanted, or even what Archie Neil wanted.

And sometimes Archie Neil didn't want to be part of the fight, slipping down onto his belly from his knees and hands, giving up any effort to drag his body by his hands. He lay limp, in a sweat, his face on his arm.

Papa squatted across the room from him.

"You will walk if you want to. The doctor said you could outgrow this. You start by crawling."

"I can't," he said, crying. He was tired. His back throbbed and his leg joints hurt.

Tonight, Angus, Willie D., Danny, Roddy, and Jack all watched, now and then offering suggestions and encouragement. But he hated being watched, he hated everyone, he hated himself, and he hated everything.

"Go away!" They left the doorway. He wanted to call Momma, she would put a stop to this if he kept crying.

But he did not call Momma. Part of him wanted what Papa wanted and made him ashamed to give up. He knew Papa loved him, but he could not do what he was asking him to do. He didn't move from his position, but glanced up at Papa to see if there was pity in his face, permission to stop the struggle.

Instead, there was disappointment. "Too bad," Papa said. "You like being in bed all the time?"

"No"—a muffled answer.

"You want to be there, in bed, when you are a grown-up man?"

"No." Archie Neil tightened a fist under his cheek and thought of hateful Great-Aunt Lizzy with her two canes and Crippled Tom in his wheelbarrow.

"You want Momma and Papa to carry you around like a sack of beans when you are a big boy of ten like Roddy? Or nearly a grown-up man like Jack? You want your sisters feeding you and dressing you when you are as old as your Papa?" His father bent over him and grabbed hold of him with both hands and gave him one hard shake.

"NO!" Archie Neil screamed. Papa had never done this before. No one was this mean to him.

"Leave me alone!" he said, crying harder.

Archie Neil had seen a dog once, running with a companion dog, hit by the wheels of a carriage. It tumbled over and over, then lay still for a moment as if dead. The other dog barked and frisked around him, and the hurt dog opened his eyes and heaved his front body upright, to romp again, but the back was broken and the hind legs remained sideways and useless. He looked at them as if surprised, and then dragged the broken luggage for several yards until the driver of the carriage took pity and killed him with a heavy stone.

"All right." Papa stood up, took his pipe from his shirt pocket, filled it with plug tobacco, and lit it. He was crying when he

17

went out on the front porch. Archie Neil heard the creak of his chair when he sat down to help Momma cut potatoes for planting. They did not say anything to each other.

Birdsong drifted from outside, and Archie Neil snuffed the spring air through the screened door. Bright light suffused the room even though it was now early evening. Through the screen, he could see a patch that included a hill with bushes and trees in slanted sunshine, all softened by a mist that he knew was beginning to hover over the river. The river would be a little sleepy now, after its first roar of spring. He was sleepy too, and he lay still. Willie D. and Roddy, as they walked across the road towards the river, spoke of fishing trout tomorrow; someone whistled far away; his sister Christy hummed as she planted flower seeds in front of the porch. Angus and Danny were playing baseball with the Coady children next door.

He could not be with them; it was all going by without him. He could not define what he meant by "it," but "it" was all out there, with people who could walk. He began to pound his fist softly against the floor, his jaw clenched tight, and as he pounded against the "it" he whispered to himself. "He'll never walk. He'll never walk. He'll never walk a step. Never. Never. Never. Sack of beans. Sack of beans. Do you like it? Sack of beans."

Archie Neil pulled up his legs under him with a wrenching effort, and fought with his body to make it crawl across the room to the screen door.

"Papa," he said, "I want to come out."

CHAPTER 3

Summer came to Margaree Forks when an American motorcar rolled down the dirt road from the direction of Chéticamp like an emperor on a tour of state. It was a shiny new 1914 Landau Coupe, gleaming black with fine white striped markings, nickel plated spoked wheels and sidelamps with cut glass. The front of the car was open, displaying glossy leather upholstery, and the closed back cab contained two well-dressed passengers. What riveted Archie Neil, strapped to his chair on the front porch, was the chauffeur, a black man, handsome and proud, sitting splendid and dignified in his uniform and leather cap. He was a man who had seen the world, who went away and came home and made big money. In a few moments, the magnificent vehicle turned the corner at the Forks, and was gone forever.

Weeks later, Archie Neil was still shifting gears. With a barrel hoop in his hands, he sat behind the wheel of a Landau Coupe. His kitchen chair took him to Germany and Austria, wherever the World War was. He planned to find out more about Archduke Ferdinand and his wife Sophie, murdered in their motorcar. And then he was planning to tour the West.

Talk of the West was in the air as much as talk of the war. To Archie Neil, West was a place of gigantic farms, mines, and lumber camps, a wonderful place of great riches. Angus MacLennan and some of the Coadys had come home for a visit, and they got Papa talking about work out West. Angus MacLennan made as much as sixty-five dollars a month. Last school term

Papa taught at Scotsville, Jack taught at Frizzleton, and Christena taught at Big Brook—and the three together did not make that much money.

So the Chisholms talked among themselves about going West and the money they could send home. But Momma would have none of it. "What good is money," she wanted to know, "if the family is broken?" They'd answer that it was just for awhile, maybe a year.

"I know better," she said. "People who go away find different lives and they don't come back."

Papa pointed out that Momma had been to Boston before their marriage, had kept house for a wealthy family up there— and where would he be today if she had not come back? Momma did not like Papa's argument. Then, if she was knitting in the evening, the stitches would come all wrong, and she would go to bed. Archie Neil still slept in their bedroom and heard her weep.

Momma knew that it was something they had made up their minds to do, and she knew that none of her family would go away against her wishes. So finally she said, "I won't stand in your way," and Papa hugged her, and she turned away to hide her face and to finish washing the dishes.

It was settled. They would leave on the train in August for Saskatchewan. Papa would teach in a place called Coblenz and board in a sod cabin with a man named Fellows; Christy would teach in Grayson, and Jack in a place called Mazenod.

The night before Papa and Jack and Christy went out West, Papa took Archie Neil to Mederic LeBlanc's to buy a length of brown wool-and-cotton tweed for Momma. She was going to make an outfit for Angus to start school, and one for Archie Neil even though he was not.

An early August storm was heading up the coast, marking the end of summer as the American motorcar had marked its beginning. When they started for the store in the wagon, the sky was overcast and wind came in cold gusts, but the rain still held off. Blue showed through the fast scudding clouds and there seemed time to get to the store and back home.

Mederic's was actually an ordinary house, the downstairs converted into a storeroom.

20

Archie Neil rode in on Papa's back. The air was warm and thick with the tobbacco smoke and kerosene and heat from the Quebec Heater. Mederic LeBlanc seemed to be in good cheer. A small, dapper man, he usually wore a tan derby and liked to have an unlit cigar in his mouth. He smiled to Archie Neil around his cigar.

A fisherman, Ready Jack Comeau, hopped off a pile of horse rugs on the counter, giving his seat to Archie Neil. Papa backed to the counter to put him down, but he was whisked up by Johnny Angus Allan MacDonald from South West Margaree, who greeted him with a big laugh and rubbed the child's face with his thick mustache, telling Archie Neil that he'd better grow one like that soon or Johnny Angus would just have to grow one for him. He plunked Archie Neil back down on the horse rugs. Archie Neil could hold himself upright with his hands but his thin, toneless legs just dangled over the counter, the left foot turned out.

Mederic said, "I am glad to see you, Archie Neil," and gave him a piece of barley candy.

"You growed like a weed, Curly," Ready Jack observed. "Before you know, you be six feet tall like your Momma, eh?"

"Show Jack them muscles," Peter Pat Coady said. He was Archie Neil's godfather. "We got a boxer here, boys, you wait and see."

This pleased Archie Neil. He rolled over onto an elbow and he pushed up his sleeve. He had developed a respectable little muscle by pulling himself around on the floor.

"He throws a mean punch for seven," Papa said, jabbing at the air. Archie Neil drew himself up straighter on his hands.

Ready Jack settled next to Papa on a pile of roofing shingles and said that maybe tomorrow wouldn't be such a good day to start the journey West.

Papa agreed that this was indeed one of the earliest August storms that anyone remembered, probably a portent of a bad winter. And Mederic told him to enjoy it, that there would not be many storms at sea in Saskatchewan.

"This night," Ready Jack said, "it remind me of a true story. One day in August ten-twelve year ago, there was a bad storm like this one, and there were three men on a boat."

21

Archie Neil listened closely, not only for the story, but for Ready Jack's rich Acadian accent. He was getting pretty good at imitating the sound of people who came to the house. Ready Jack told the well-known story of three fishermen who said the rosary as they rowed through a terrible storm, way off Cape Mabou.

"They were out of sight of land. A storm came up. At first they weren't a bit afraid, but when their boat seem to come close to be foundering, they began to take stock of their past. And probably some of it wasn't just according to the sheet they'd like to see up there in Heaven when they died.

"So they prayed at the top of their voices, just sure they were going to die. They were saying the rosary and trying to row the boat. And this one fellow was appealing to the Lord in every way that he could. He was promising the Lord everything. He said, 'Dear Lord, if you'll take us out of this trough that we're in now—I'll never chase another girl.' And the other two agreed to do the same, to give up women if only God would save them.

"But the storm only got worse.

"So another one of the fishermen promised to never miss Mass, and again they all agreed. If the Lord would save them from this terrible storm, all three of them would never miss Mass again.

"Okay. But even this didn't help. The storm was just ripping away.

"Then the third fellow said that if the Lord would save him from this awful, awful storm, he would never drink another drop of booze.

"But the man at the tiller cut him short. 'Don't promise Him that for me, you fool!' he shouted. 'I think I see Margaree Island!'"

The men all laughed with Ready Jack, but then Ready Jack shook his head and leaned back with a solemn air.

"But you know, I did see two men drown in a storm like this one. They was loaded with salt to bring to the fish plant at Terre Noire. Boat went down. I saw them go down. Strange thing is that two-three years before, I saw lights off the point, God help me if I'm lyin'. You tell 'em, Malcolm."

"It's true," shouted Malcolm the Post, a very deaf man. "I

saw lights too. So did half the people down that way. They said it was only gas."

"Hot air, most likely," said Peter Pat.

"Maybe ball lightning or something like that," Papa added.

"No, it wasn't. It was a light. And I could see a boat in the light, clear as day. Same boat as went down after."

"A forerunner," Malcolm confirmed, first checking with Ready Jack's lips as he talked, to make sure they were still on the same topic. "A forerunner. Heard same kind of thing over to Cap Le Moine and Belle Côte. Crowds on beaches seen when there was no one there; then a ship wrecked after in the same place. And crowds gathered to take the bodies from the sea—the same crowd they were seeing in that place for years and years before."

Then Ready Jack took his time telling the story about an unknown ship found in perfect condition adrift offshore from Chéticamp, no one on board. It was first seen just before daylight, and there was an eerie blue light around it, and it so spooked those who approached to claim salvage that they dared not touch it. They would not put a rope aboard.

Then the next day, just like that, it was gone.

By now, Archie Neil forgot that they were in a store and not on board a doomed fishing boat. He felt spirits in that storeroom as tangible as the men he listened to. He felt a sense of awe in the bravery of the fishermen who went to sea despite lurking evil spirits and the storms of August. And he wished he could tell a story, too.

That made him think about his sister Christy. She was probably his favourite storyteller. And she was leaving tomorrow with Papa and Jack.

Earlier that day, Archie Neil had crawled over to Christy's trunk to see what she was going to take on the train to the West. It dawned on him that Christy was not coming back, and a kind of hollow alarm attached to every item Momma meticulously folded and put into the trunk.

Sitting on the floor, he rested his head on his arm on the chair seat, and just watched.

He thought Christy looked beautiful. She tried on the blouse Momma had just finished, came out to show it, her eyes full of delight. It was a perfect fit, as delicate as the finest in Eaton's catalogue, made of something Momma had called Georgette, silky blue and hand embroidered.

He loved Christy as much as he loved Momma and Papa. Christy had once walked ten miles in the rain in the middle of the week from where she was teaching near Big Brook, just to get home for his birthday. She brought three books for his very own, all by Horatio Alger—*Ragged Dick*, *Luck and Pluck*, and *Tattered Tom*—and she read them to him, every word. Archie Neil certainly liked Tattered Tom. Tattered Tom was honest and courageous and he worked hard, and people came to recognize him and he overcame being poor and everything else put in his way.

Sometimes Christy told him stories about Cyclops and Vulcan and the Arabian Nights.

Now, he could read for himself, skipping over the things that were too hard. There were many words at which he guessed, because there seemed to be more words in books than the words people used when they talked. And when he tried to use book words, people usually laughed. One day Papa was impressed when Archie Neil read most of a typewritten letter International Harvester had sent to Jack. Archie Neil informed Papa that it was in answer to Jack's application for a job selling farm machinery and that while there were no openings they would keep his name in their files.

These days, Archie Neil wanted to hang on to Papa, to touch him, because he too was definitely going away to a far place.

Also, this thing they called a World War worried him.

There was a pause. Malcolm the Post observed that the MacDonald's chewing tobacco had far more juice in it than Pictou Twist. That led to some debate. Then quiet.

Archie Chisholm was going away.

"I'll tell you fellows a story," Papa said. "When I'm gone it'll be winter. And you'll think it's cold. But you'll remember this little story. And you'll know you're not so cold. It'll keep you fellows warm till I get home.

"One of the old-time hotels in Inverness was noted for how you'd suffer with cold in the winter. There was very little heat.

"In those days, when you stayed at the hotel overnight, it was usually to go out on the morning train at seven-thirty.

"There was always notice given to an old gentleman by the name of John R. MacDonald who used to pick up the passengers at the hotel and also pick up their luggage—take them to the train.

"One particular night this traveller was in one of the rooms and it was extremely cold. He got up around seven o'clock in the morning. It was snowing and extremely frosty.

"Of course, Mr. MacDonald had one of those great big handlebar moustaches. And he had driven down from home with his horse and sleigh, to pick up the passengers. And the icicles had formed on his moustache. He came into the dining room with the icicles hanging, pretty near frozen.

"And the traveller was just finishing his breakfast. And he looked at Mr. MacDonald, and he asked him, 'Excuse me,' he said, 'but which room did you sleep in last night?'"

They had a good laugh over that, and Malcolm the Post said that that was as true as he was sitting there. And then Ready Jack said to Papa, "I'll give you something else—keep you warm." He pulled a flask out of his coat pocket. Ready Jack took a quick drink and offered it around. Most of the men took a drink but Papa declined. Then Ready Jack took Papa into the back room with Peter Pat to look at pole straps and martingales, and Archie Neil saw Papa's shadow on the far wall, the bottle tipped up.

By now it was quite dark outside, and the rain slashed at the front windows, and the men felt even less disposed to leave the light and warmth. They talked on. After a while Paddy Gillis said to Papa, "Remember back two years ago, Archie. We was settin' right here talkin' about the election. Guessin' who voted for who. And your Uncle John knew how everybody voted. But ask him how he knew and he says, 'Only the man above knows.' 'Only the man above knows.' But I swear till the paint peels off this store, that he knew every damn vote."

Papa knocked the ashes out of his pipe, filled it and re-lit. "Now," he said, "since we're all friends here—and since I'm going away tomorrow—I'll tell you.... You'll remember that the polling booth was at my Grandfather Chisholm's, right?"

Everyone agreed.

"The voting table was in a corner, with a blanket hung around it, right? No one could look in." Agreed.

"All right. Uncle John just had to know who was voting for who. So he had cut a little hole in the floor above the polling table. And he watched."

"Now, Archie, I don't think so," Peter Pat said. "I talked to John myself off and on that day."

"Oh, he didn't bother with the big Liberals and Tories. He knew them. It was the questionables that got his attention. He'd slip upstairs when they came to vote, lay flat on the floor with his eye to the hole."

Ready Jack burst out laughing. "So that's how he knew I voted Liberal!"

"And all you other fence sitters," Paddy said. "You all say you voted for whoever won the election."

"It is healthier on the fence. Keep the politicians guessing, an' they are nicer to you after the election, is it not so?"

There was a pause. All of them knew stories about family men who lost jobs after elections because they voted for the wrong party.

"So, you see," Papa said, "the man above did know."

A rumbling of thunder and a hard drive of wind against the building brought them back to thoughts of an unpleasant trip home, but they got ready to leave. Mederic measured the cloth for Momma, wrapped it in newspaper and tied it with string. They said brief goodbyes to Archie Chisholm. Then Ready Jack noticed the end of the wrapping string hanging over the edge of the counter, attached to a huge spool. Very casually, he tied the end of the string to his own coat button. Mederic did not notice, but the others saw. Ready Jack passed Archie Neil with a wink. "See you later, Curly"—and he left the store for the two-mile walk to his house.

For a minute no one said anything. But Archie Neil did not see much fun in that. "Mr. LeBlanc," he said, pointing to the floor, "what's happening to your string?"

Mederic came over the counter like a cat. He saw it sliding over the floor, moving the sawdust like a column of ants, and going out under the door. He didn't understand it, and opened the door, groping around outside in the dark rain for the string.

"Ready Jack is gone," Papa said. "I think it must have tangled in his coat."

Mederic started on a run after Ready Jack, hollering at the top of his voice, over the sound of the rain and over the laughter behind him.

Papa held Archie Neil the whole time they waited on the platform in Inverness. Listening to Papa during the long drive from Margaree Forks, Archie Neil had decided that Inverness was on the very edge of the world. Riding through the town confirmed that the ocean was at its feet; that there were whole streets of two-family houses all shaped the same and all the same colour, all owned by the coal company; and that there were more stores and more people moving about than Archie Neil had seen anywhere except at a parish picnic.

The railroad station was crowded. Momma, Jack, and Christy stood with them, awkward, saying last-minute things. The wait got very long. Archie Neil thought Christy looked the prettiest of any girl there, in her blue blouse and skirt and her velveteen sailor hat.

Then, two hours late, the Judique Flyer came in. Archie Neil had fallen asleep but he was up now. First a faint rumbling, then the black coal plume; and as it approached Archie Neil heard an answering rumble behind his breastbone. He saw Cyclops, the black iron giant bellowing, a Vulcan forging thunderbolts on Etna. He wanted to tell Christy, but she was nervously tucking a wisp of hair under her hat, saying goodbye. His breath quickened as the long whistle sounded, the bell on Cyclops' back clanged, and the beast slowed down, venting clouds of steam, stopping and then swallowing people.

Archie Neil saw the engineer leaning out of the window in a grey striped denim cap with a long bill, really a monarch.

Papa carried Archie Neil up the iron steps for a brief look at the rows of seats inside the train. The car smelled like tar and tobacco. Then he gave him a bear hug and told him to be a good boy and to be a help to Momma, and Archie Neil promised that he would. Papa took Archie Neil down and handed him to Momma. Momma took him and kissed Jack and Christy, and he did too, and Momma cried when she kissed Papa and

Papa cried too, and then Archie Neil really started to cry. The luggage had disappeared. Christy was holding lunches for everyone. The train chugged and wheezed and ground into motion, and Momma and Archie Neil were left on the platform.

It was a long ride home. Archie Neil felt he had been to the edge of the world, beyond which was only the West and the World War, and now Christy and Papa and Jack. He felt frightened and abandoned. And Archie Neil decided that the only good thing about going to Inverness was that he made up his mind, definitely, that instead of a chauffeur, he was going to be a railroad engineer.

CHAPTER 4

September was a beginning for Angus, and an ending for Archie Neil. On the first day of school Archie Neil watched from Momma's arms as Angus walked proudly down the dirt road of Margaree Forks, a handsome, straight-limbed boy, tall for his age. He attached one hand to Roddy's and in the other he carried his own lunch tin. He wore a brown suit, straight cut knee pants and long stockings, a matching coat with a buckle belt and diagonal pockets, all of which Momma had made, supervised stitch by stitch by Archie Neil, who insisted on having a duplicate suit for himself.

But Archie Neil was not going to school. The bitterness of this rankled in him all through last school year when he should have started, and now again. Now even Angus was gone through the day. Angus was going to school with Roddy and Willie D. and Danny and the girls, where interesting things happened and there were things to learn and homework to do. He was being left behind. He understood that he couldn't skate or play ball. But school sounded like something you could almost do without legs.

In a way, school had been coming to Archie Neil. The children often practised their recitations at the foot of Archie Neil's bed. The *Hesperus* was wrecked at the foot of that bed and John Moore's body was buried in the middle of the road under cover of night.... Archie Neil was a splendid audience—captive and interested and quick to tell them when they were speaking the

29

lines in a way that made no sense. He was learning the poems himself and enjoyed playing the teacher.

But that was at nighttime and at the foot of his bed. He still wanted to go to school. He wanted to know why he wasn't good enough to go. He pulled this thought deep into himself, weeping bitterly, mad at God and Momma and his crooked legs and the twisted foot that left him behind. His legs and back continued to hurt him.

He cried through that first morning without Angus in the house, then he slept. In the afternoon, he re-read the last instalment of "Blue Water," a serial story in the *Journal Bulletin*, a Port Hastings paper. It was a good story, and he was impatient for the next part.

When everybody came home from school, Archie Neil dragged himself into the kitchen to pump information out of Angus about school but Angus had found a new friend at school and they were going out to play. The others had chores, their own friends, homework. Archie Neil was delighted when Angus brought friends home, because sometimes they would include him or take him outside to watch them play.

That same September, Archie Neil began to give Momma a very hard time about going to church. He would be sick just before Sunday Mass, or balky and difficult, sometimes creating such an uproar that his brothers and sisters left early in disgust.

"What is wrong with you?" Momma asked.

Archie Neil sullenly reached for the book he had been reading, and did not answer, but Momma was adamant this time.

"I'm too big," he finally said.

She shook her head but said nothing.

"Everybody—" he faltered. "They all stare at me. I don't—" He looked at her defiantly. He was angry. "I don't want you to carry me." Sack of beans, he thought. "I'm too big."

"But how else—?"

"I won't go! I won't."

"Yes, you will," she said.

Momma said that religion was not negotiable. She did not like even little infractions, such as when Granduncle Jack Chisholm said grace before a Sunday dinner. If he liked what was on the menu he made a big sign of the cross, the proper piety of forehead, breast, shoulder and shoulder. But when they were having salt herring and turnips, it was just a token flutter of a limp wrist. This infuriated Momma.

And a clergyman's visit for dinner was an event she prepared for days. None of the boys dared to keep a cap on when a clergyman passed on the road. Denomination made no difference to Momma. Minister or priest, she expected them to be respectful.

So Momma and Archie Neil remained at loggerheads about church, and usually Momma won out. She carried him in, sort of dangling him at her side. But he convinced her to sit at the back.

Otherwise, he tried to follow through on his promise to Papa to help her and to be good, and he found it satisfying to wash dishes, hanging perched on a chair with the chairback under his armpits, or scrubbing the spruce floor white with sand, or churning butter, peeling potatoes. At times the house was his prison, at times his castle, as he crawled from room to room, to put things in order or to find lost gold or to go through his brothers' and sisters' belongings.

He'd get Momma to stop work by asking for songs, or they'd work together and she'd sing. One day she sang a new song that she learned at Chimney Corner, about the MacIntoshes who had the devil's time slaughtering their pig. Archie Neil was having a miserable day—his legs hurt and he wanted to be in school and he wanted Papa—so Momma squinted up her eyes and became the pig and sang out in Gaelic: "'Murder!' he yells, 'What a son of a witch you are. I'm going to die today, but you'll suffer yet. If my relatives find out, there will be blood before we part. I hope you don't live long. You'll be here in the woods of St. Rose, and I will be served at a table in Halifax.'" Momma sang it to the air of "The Cuckoo's Nest" and put them both in good cheer.

One night Willena was helping Roddy with his reading for school. They were baffled by a question: Who was The Old Woman of Threadneedle Street? Archie Neil stirred on the rug in the living room, listening to them, astonished. He knew!

"The Bank of England," he said. In his mind he saw an old woman who for some reason gave money to people on a river bank in England, whether England was a province or a country.

"Well, I don't believe it," Willena said.

But the next day, the teacher said that Archie Neil was right, and Willena came home and told everybody and Archie Neil felt brilliant. And to prove his smartness, he paid more attention to everybody's homework, even read their books. He said it was better than going to school.

He listened to them practise recitations. Roddy was memorizing parts of a long poem called "The Lady of the Lake." He had to recite a portion in class each Friday.

"Sir Walter Scott got the story from his grandmother," Roddy told to Archie Neil. "Teacher said Sir Walter Scott was lame. Maybe he had polio too."

This galvanized Archie Neil's attention, and he listened with avidity as Roddy and Willena read about the outlawed Lord Douglas, and Fitz-James and his hopeless love for Ellen, and the murderous Roderick Dhu—about lurking spies and burning beacons and swift-riding messengers, the prophecies of hermit monks and the ring-favours of kings.

This glorious story came from a cripple like himself.

Isabel MacLennan Chisholm—Momma

Archie A. Chisholm—Papa, with
Dougald MacKenzie and Archie Neil

Christena
Chisholm
Pillar (Christy)

Jack Chisholm

Mary Ann Chisholm

Margaree Harbour School

1930 Visit Home: Donald (Danny) with Willie D.; Willena with her husband Mike Murphy

Roddy Chisholm

Angus, Donald, & Archie Neil
Archie Neil and a friend

View of Margaree River

Johnny Stephen White

Left: Papa with
Peter Pat Coady, 1937

Angus Chisholm fiddling

Momma on the front porch, 1930's

Isabel (Archie Neil's niece),
Archie Neil, and a friend

Willie D. with Angus & Archie Neil's first fiddle, plus one

Left: Papa at the family home, with Donald, Isabel, and Angus

Above right: annual Conservative meeting, Halifax, with Sen. Clem O'Leary, Archie Neil, A. R. MacNeil, Bob MacLellan

Archie Neil, teacher, with students at Belle Côte School, 1956

CHAPTER 5

Archie Neil clung to the edges of the coasting sled as his brothers pulled him over the frozen hillocks of grassy snow on the margin, then out over the roof of hard ice that capped the Margaree River.

Angus and Danny took turns pulling him, only one of them skating at a time because they had to share the one pair of skates. The skates clamped onto their shoes. Archie Neil tried them on before they left the house, a silly, useless thing to do, but it felt good, a novelty, like going outside late at nighttime. Momma bundled him and he was warm and gloriously happy. Now and then, one of the Coady or MacLennan or MacKinnon boys took over for Danny and Angus, and those boys, not being under Momma's constraints, were goaded by Archie Neil into pulling him faster and faster, making wide turns in which the sled slid sideways or zinged over bumps in the ice. Archie Neil loved the speed, but those rides were usually cut short if Roddy or Willena noticed.

Older boys and girls skated in pairs or in small groups and Simon MacKinnon from the Shore Road tagged along wherever Willena was, and John Simon MacDonald haunted the group around Mary Ann.

Archie Neil thought Willena took ridiculous care, trying to be stylish just to go skating. She wore a made-over coat, new to her, and a matching hat with black fur trim. Every year, a cousin in Boston sent down a box of winter clothes. They seldom

33

fit, but they were up-to-date and in good condition and Momma was clever at sewing.

Today, Willena wore a black muff made out of something called Manchurian Dog, trimmed with a head, a tail, and two paws. Momma said the outfit was "smart," but Archie Neil and Angus agreed that wearing a dead dog was disgusting. Mary Ann did not think so, she wanted a share of the muff. Mary Ann got to wear it to church most Sundays.

Even Roddy and Willie D. dressed up when there were girls around, and Archie Neil and Angus spied on their tendency to pair off, satirizing their behaviour and stupid conversations. They saw now that the phenomenon was not localized with the Chisholms but that it was really an epidemic. There was a lot of teasing and chasing and laughing and couples skating off alone. There had been no dances in the church halls since Advent, the beginning of December, but it was the general view that skating was better than a dance for courting.

There were a number of cutters and even wagons on the river, bright lanterns burning, couples bundled in buffalo robes. The river was a winter highway. Archie Neil heard Momma say that Joe Coady, the brother of Moses, took a load of heavy timber onto the river ice at his place two miles up on the Southwest and drove the team clear to Margaree Harbour.

Gradually, the boys lost interest in pulling the sled. They were having great fun racing or forming chains of skaters who pivoted in great circles, trying to shake off the skater on the outer end. The Coady boys had four hockey sticks and a puck they were willing to share, and a small cheering crowd watched the players.

Archie Neil was beginning to get cold, sitting on the sled on the periphery of the skaters. A wind had come up which the others did not notice, for they were heated with activity, but he felt it keenly. His feet and legs ached, and his back was exacting vengeance after the bumpy rides. Little whirls of powdery snow whipped from the surface of the ice, stinging his face. He pulled his toque down and hunkered deeper into his coat.

Angus skated up to him at a great speed, at the last minute turning sideways, scraping up the ice with the broadside of his blades and coming to a stop.

"They're gonna let me play hockey!" he said, "Next turn! Watch me!"

"I'm cold," Archie Neil said. "Take me up home."

"Yah. In awhile. As soon as I'm finished."

He skated off. Later, Archie Neil called to Mary Ann, but she was talking with some girls and did not hear him.

He began to shiver. His hands were stiff in his mitts, stumps.

After a few more minutes, Willie D. came by and asked if he wanted another ride.

"Take me up home," Archie Neil said. "I'm cold."

"Aw, come on," he said. "We're having fun. I'll give you a ride, and you'll feel better, wait and see."

He gave him a fast ride, and then joined with a group who were skating in a long chain trying to bridge the whole river. The ride made Archie Neil colder. His breath was making ice on his muffler, and his face was stinging and stiff.

A half hour later, Roddy left his girlfriend to check on him.

"How ya doin,' sport?" he asked, kindly. He put his hand on Archie Neil's shoulder. Archie Neil did not reply, it seemed that even his mouth was too cold, and when Roddy looked closer, he said, "Oh, my God."

"You're lucky it wasn't worse," Momma scolded. Roddy carried another kettle of warm water from the stove to the galvanized washtub. Archie Neil was shivering violently, his legs and feet screaming with pain. He didn't want to cry, and he didn't want Roddy in any more trouble. That was the last time he went sledding.

Now that he was again sharing a room upstairs with Angus, Archie Neil bumped down the stairs each morning on the seat of his pants.

When he reached the landing, instead of sliding on down, he grabbed the railing and pulled himself upright, standing. He had been doing this for some time now. His legs wavered with the strain but he stood there and tried to take a step—but he could not lift the left foot at all, and only the heel of the right foot. Any effort to move his feet or to stand unaided dropped him down hard on his backside and he was frightened of falling, almost equal to his aversion about being watched. Sometimes he could stand holding onto the back of a chair, and he moved around the kitchen sliding the chair. The carpet in the parlour was like a closed door.

One day, Angus and Roddy were in the entry shed, just home from school, when they heard a crash and a yelp of astonishment. They rushed into the kitchen to find Archie Neil standing in the middle of the kitchen in his stocking feet. The chair he had been using was on its side on the floor.

None of them could believe that he was standing unaided, least of all Archie Neil. "Take a step!" Roddy said. His legs wavered, the knees threatening to unlock, the strain making his face clammy with sweat.

His feet were positioned crossways on the uneven planks of the softwood floor, and a tiny rise prevented him from sliding his foot. "I can't!" he said. "Roddy, you got to help me get down!"

"No," Roddy countered. "Take a step."

"I'm scared," he said. Pains ran up his legs, and his left foot cramped. "I can't lift my foot over the bump."

"Angus and I will help you," Roddy said, seeing Archie Neil's problem. They grasped his arms on each side of him, and turned him around so that his feet could glide in the direction of the planks. They let go for a moment and he managed to slide one foot in front of the other twice before the knees gave way and they caught him.

But they could not induce him to try again.

When Momma had company, Archie Neil often made a brief appearance in the doorway, scooting beside some chair so that no one would see him dragging himself. He never liked to be found on the floor. He loved to listen to the women who visited. They had no idea how closely he followed their conversations about who was pregnant, or wanted to be, or should not be; and, afterwards, he and Angus discussed how the process might work. Barnyard animals provided some graphic clues, but the boys were not sure how much of this carried over to humans. Human courting seemed silly enough, and it was impossible to imagine the women who visited Momma or the suited men in church, doing what the animals did. However, since most of them had progeny, they presumed that something was accomplished. It was very stimulating to the imagination.

"Remember Mrs. MacKinnon, the midwife?" Momma asked Rebecca Coady in the parlour one afternoon. Rebecca nodded with a smile. Archie Neil knew Momma's tone. He stood there in the doorway and did not move or make a sound. He didn't want to be shooed away. It was going to be a story. If it was a good one, he'd tell it upstairs later. It would be something fresh to win attention, when they were telling him about things that happened at school. He knew how good stories worked. So he just held onto a chair and tried to be the chair and drank up the story.

"Well, years ago," Momma said, pulling her knitting into her lap, "Mrs. MacKinnon went to help this couple having their first baby. Dhia, but they were poor—not much of anything. Just cut up old clothes for the new baby, barely enough for themselves to wear or to eat in the house. And it was a winter night and the girl, Hughena, she was in pain and she told Murdoch to go get Mrs. MacKinnon. He was as scared as she was. Murdoch was no good to her at all, all nerves.

"When Mrs. MacKinnon got there, the fire was out and there was nothing in the house but one lantern to see by. So she got Murdoch to clean the globe, and she got the mother ready to give birth.

"Mrs. MacKinnon told Murdoch to hold the lantern so she could see, and sure enough come a baby boy, big and healthy. Now, Murdoch was a happy man to have a son to help out on the farm.

"Mrs. MacKinnon slapped the baby and cut the cord, and she wrapped him up in a piece of blanket.

"But Hughena was still in pain. Murdoch held up the lantern. And another baby came into the lamp light. This time a girl. Well, Murdoch was happy still, though he was worried about managing with two. But he had a fine boy and now a girl.

"But no sooner was the girl wrapped and warm, when Hughena made another fuss about the pains—and a triplet, another girl, was born. Och, the only triplets ever around here. Murdoch was shaking with the lantern now, and was steppin' back. Mrs. MacKinnon told him to come in closer, she needed the light.

"'Dhia, Dhia,' Murdoch said. 'I'm going to blow out this damn lantern. I think it's the light that's drawing them!'"

Rebecca laughed. And moved right in with, "Well, poor Murdoch." Then she started in: "I had a friend and she and her husband were married for a few years and didn't have any luck at all having babies. A visiting priest—I think it was Father John Angus—come one day and said, 'I'm going to Rome next month, and when I go, I'm going to have a special candle lit for your intention. I'll pray that you'll have a family.'"

"Did it work?" Momma asked.

"Well. He did as he promised. And my friend got pregnant that month. After that, there was new babies every year for eight years, some of them twins. And Father John Angus was visiting her this day. When he got to their lane, all he could see was a great string of diapers on the line, and her washing diapers in a big tub on the porch. While they were talking, he asked about her husband.

"'Oh, he's not here,' she said. 'He's gone. He went on a trip,' she said, 'to Rome. To blow out that damned candle you lit there eight years ago.'"

On Christmas Eve all the Chisholms, all except Momma and Archie Neil, went to Midnight Mass. Momma boiled a big pot of blue potatoes. And she also boiled two of the isbean in their casings, punching the sausages with a fork to let the air out. When the family got home, about two-thirty in the morning, the house was filled with spicy aromas and they had a big feed with huge slices of hot mince pie for dessert. They were happy enough, but it wasn't the same without Papa.

They had a tree decorated with dried cranberries and silver ornaments made from tea wrappers, ready for Santa Claus. T. Eaton's catalogue had a spring-wound cast iron train that moved on a track, and this was what Archie Neil wanted for Christmas. It cost $2.25. He knew it was unlikely he would get it, whether he was good or bad. He thought Santa Claus was a miserly old fraud, but tried to maintain a positive attitude, just in case.

He didn't get the toy train. What he did get was a pair of crutches carved by Peter Pat Coady. But he refused to try them while anyone was watching. When he did test them they felt clumsy; they hurt his armpits and wobbled, good for making him fall, he thought, and nothing else.

But Peter Pat came over one afternoon and he was a lot like Papa when he made up his mind.

"Don't put your weight on the armpits," he said, watching Archie Neil clump across the kitchen. The rest of the family had been banished from the room. "Those crosspieces can hold your weight. Use your hands and arms and shoulders. You're strong as an ox in the shoulders. Come on now, try it."

Peter Pat was right. But it still felt awkward. "Divide your weight between the crutches and your feet," he advised. "Then move the crutches ahead, swing your body, move the crutches, swing. You'll get the hang of it."

It worked! Archie Neil's heart suddenly raced with excitement. He was walking! swinging back and forth across the kitchen.

"Now get me a nice cup of hot tea from the stove," Peter Pat said, "on your way by."

Archie Neil looked at him with disbelief.

"Next time," Peter Pat said, rumpling his hair.

"Yah," he answered, grinning. "Next time."

CHAPTER 6

It was a brilliant September morning with the smells of autumn in the the air and trees touched with yellow and red reflected in the river. Through the last weeks of summer, Archie Neil thought constantly about this day; he was going to go to school. At last he would be just like all the other kids. They would all be his friends. He would join them in complaining about homework even though he loved it; he would have fun; he would read things like "Lady of the Lake." It was going to be great.

Ida, the brown mare, arrived at the school yard carrying a nervous Archie Neil, his tin of sandwiches, his can of tea, and his crutches. As soon as he appeared students stopped to watch him dismount. Archie Neil heard someone say, "There's that Chisholm kid. He's mental." Angus was on the far side of the horse to help him. Archie Neil leaned over.

"They're staring at me!" he said in a tight whisper. "Tell them to get away from here!"

"Just give me the crutches and the lunch, and get down." Angus also whispered.

"I'm going home," Archie Neil said, panic rising. He grabbed at the reins to turn the horse. "They're staring at me."

"Don't be so stupid," Angus said, his own patience wearing thin. He yanked the reins from his brother. "Get down, now! I don't have all day. I have to take Ida home, and walk back. You're a friggin' pain. So shut up and get down."

"If they come near me, I'll clobber them."

He finally slid down on the far side of Ida, and Angus mounted and started off for home. Archie Neil looked at the students with a warning scowl. He should have got off closer to the school. Then he worried about going into the wrong one of the two classrooms. Which one had Grade 3? At least he was to be among those his own age.

Momma had made him new long pants from an old pair of Jack's. She'd left them full at the knees, but nothing could hide his skinny, funny-looking legs. His left foot turned out ninety degrees. He felt awkward and shabby. His clothes were not new. And he was sure they could see his terrible legs.

Archie Neil lurched forward and hunched across the school yard on his crutches. He wanted to bellow at them. As long as he could use his arms, he could climb anything, he could vault a fence better than any of them. He could control his descent and could come down lightly on his crippled legs.

Then he thought of falling in front of everybody. The thought was a horror. He was tough, but he always had bruises somewhere from falls. The thought made him sweat with dread. Falling and being stared at, or being teased—he hated them all. The pantry door home was scarred by chunks of firewood he had flung at his sisters when they laughed. Once he kept them hostage in there until he felt like letting them out. He thought of locking all of these students in the outhouse until he got into the school, safe in a chair. All he needed was some pieces of firewood. He had given warning to his own family members to stay clear of him at school, and they did.

The few yards to the schoolhouse seemed a long way. When he was almost there, a shy voice came from just behind him.

"Hi, Archie Neil. Want me to carry your lunch?"

Archie Neil seethed with instant resentment. "I'll carry my own lunch!"

He turned. It was Dougald MacKenzie, a slight elf of a boy. Papa especially liked Dougald, who was sometimes a visitor at their house. "I'm sorry, " Dougald said. "My dad told me to be nice to you." Then he said, "I don't mind."

"Here." Archie Neil looked at his friend with gratitude. It was awkward carrying things with the crutches.

A young pretty woman met them at the door.

"Hello, Dougald," she said with a smile, taking his hand and shaking it, just like he was a grown-up man. And to Archie Neil she said, "Welcome! I'm Annabel Coady, your teacher. I've been looking forward to meeting you."

He liked her instantly. Maybe school would be all right after all.

"Here comes wobble-legs!" said Bevis Dobson.

Bevis hobbled about comically, making other students laugh. This went on daily. Angus finally told Archie Neil that he was going to have to fight his own battles. The Chisholm brothers were getting tired of this. And Bevis had tough friends. Willie D. and Danny and Angus often told Bevis to shut up or they would get him, which they had actually done a few times, pounding him good. This resulted in skirmishes between the anti- and the pro-Chisholm elements in the school, with little clear resolution.

One day Angus squared off with Bevis, right in front of the school.

"Oh, I'm scared," Bevis said, adding an obscene gesture to his performance, humping around as though one foot was nailed to the ground.

Without noticing it, he came close to Archie Neil who was still astride the horse Ida, and suddenly found himself whomped on the back so hard that he landed face first. He looked up at a crutch poised and ready for a second thrust.

The next day, Bevis put on his performance well out of range, but there was less heart in it. On the way home he teased Ida, pelting her with stones. The gentle mare became desperate and almost threw her rider, something she had never done in her life.

Archie Neil no longer bothered to complain to anyone or waste words with Bevis. One day when Bevis was absorbed teasing someone else, Archie Neil swung over to him and flattened him with the broad side of a crutch, and when Bevis tried to get up, Archie Neil pinned him down with the end of it against his chest—until somebody warned him that a teacher was coming. In the arms and shoulders, he was every bit as strong as Bevis.

42

Bevis changed tactics, from open warfare to sabotage. Glue was spread on the rests of Archie Neil's crutches. Sometimes his scarf and hat were missing, and his lunch box was occasionally emptied before noon. Books and homework were scribbled with words like "mental" and "wobble-legs" and "Hunch-leg of the Forks." But these incidents eventually became rare.

It was no use telling the teacher. Archie Neil's crutches were lethal enough. Used sparingly, carefully, Annabel Coady continued to believe Archie Neil Chisholm was a saint.

By early November, Ida was accustomed to the routine. She went home by herself in the morning and Momma would let her loose again in the afternoon and most days she arrived back at school like clockwork. Some days, Angus or Willie D. had to fetch her away from tempting roadside browse. For his part, Archie Neil became an expert at vaulting onto her back and getting off without help, and he knew this impressed the older girls.

He was growing rapidly, his upper body very broad and muscular, and he was proud of this. Even his hips and legs had taken on some flesh, for he was in robust health. This meant that the long pants Momma made over in August were binding by October. He figured that underwear was dispensable. Handed down from Danny, underwear only made his pants tighter.

One breezy afternoon in early October, he vaulted onto Ida, and the girls went wild. Archie Neil sat up even straighter on Ida, hoping to further impress them with the fine figure he cut as he, and his gaping trousers, rode away.

CHAPTER 7

Papa surprised everyone in early February. One day, he simply was there hugging Momma at the doorway, lifting her off her feet, telling her he was too lonesome to stay away any longer. Watching them, Archie Neil had an idea of what their courtship may have been like and it made him want to laugh. Then he showed Papa that he could walk with crutches, and Papa's eyes filled with tears.

The next night the house was jammed with visitors. Peter Pat and his wife Rebecca were there, Alex Gillis and his sister Winnie, Sandy MacLean and Angus Allan Gillis and Angus Allan's cousin Jimmy Dubh Gillis. Johnny Stephen White was there, and Donald John Beaton the Tailor and Hughie Angus Lord MacDonald and Paddy Gillis—the most of them fiddlers, some really terrific players. Ready Jack Comeau was there early. The house was full of MacLennans and Chisholms and Gillises and Coadys, and when the chairs ran out people sat on the floor or on a stump brought in from the woodpile. Several guests brought their fiddles and a few brought bottles. Momma had biscuits and sweets and plenty of tea, and every woman came in with something to eat under a cloth or waxed paper.

Uncle Calum had his four drinks right away, then sat like a stone on the bottom step with his nose aimed at the fiddlers, and all evening long the party walked around him.

"You made your fortune in the West, Archie Chisholm," said Angus Allan, tuning. "Did you leave any for the rest of us?"

"What would you do with more money if you had it?"

"Och, I'm planning on buying North Sydney."

"That wouldn't make much of a dent in your pocket," said Ready Jack. "You better buy yourself some new tunes."

"I tried. Sandy MacLean's after stealing them all."

Momma had a crowd around her already, and she didn't mind showing off the new shoes Papa brought. There were soon so many conversations going that Archie Neil did not know where to sit to catch the best of them, so he decided to stick with the fiddlers.

"A lot of music went to Heaven this week," Papa told Johnny White. Most people called him Johnny Stephen and, like his father, he was a salmon guide on the Margaree River. He was a meticulous man, careful in dress and in the placement of every hair. He also stuttered. He liked to be on top of things and Papa's comment threw him for a second.

"W-what do you m-mean?"

"I read in the paper that Louis Fuller died," Papa said solemnly. Fuller was a fiddler that neither of them liked. He played very fast, making hodge-podge medleys from portions of mis-matched tunes, and was just no good for dancing. Not afraid of any shortcuts, he'd skip over anything difficult to play. Johnny thought of him as a destroyer of Scottish music.

In fact, he had not died; Papa was making that part up.

"I'm g-going to tell you something, Archie. If he t-took as many shortcuts going to Heaven as he did going through tunes, he'd have got to Heaven long ago."

Peter Pat couldn't resist his own jab at Johnny. Johnny was a hockey fanatic.

"I was readin' in the paper—Montreal Canadiens have an all-Irish team this year, now they joined the League. Good hockey players, them Irish."

"Yah," agreed Johnny with a laugh. "W-well, I'd like to see the newspaper you f-fellas read. La-LaLonde, La-Lavi-olette, Joliet—awful Irish, like yourselfs."

Alex Gillis, a good fiddler still in his teens, laughed at this. "Well, I read in the paper that you tied the knot, Johnny Stephen."

"I'm tellin' you Alex, I very near got the noose one time,

but I g-got away! Now, what happened was this:

"I went to a wedding down East Margaree—n-not mine, though."

And Johnny White told them the story of how he was awakened at ten o'clock at night to come and play for a wedding reception. They wore out he didn't know how many fiddlers. This may have been the second or third day they were at it. Anyhow, he went and he played three hours or so, maybe four—"p-played my heart out"—and was not offered so much as a cup of tea, much less a drink. Then somebody passed the hat, which was the way fiddlers were often paid, and when he counted the collection, it was exactly one dollar and six cents. A dollar, a nickel, and one of those enormous coppers. Johnny didn't say a word. He just packed up his fiddle and walked out of the house.

He walked six miles to his home in Fordview, in a thick, thick fog. Nobody offered to give him a lift because they were that angry he left.

"The fog was so th-thick," he said, "I could throw my hat ahead of me and p-pick it up on the way by. It was resting on the f-fog."

Hughie Angus Lord struck up the fiddle tune "The Crooked Stove Pipe," and soon the whole room was alive with the music and tapping feet. Women sat in place with backs straight and stepped out the music and softly kept rhythm with the flat of their hands on their thighs.

While he was playing, Angus Allan Gillis said to Sandy MacLean, "Now Sandy, you remember when we were in school? You were a chap then, five years older than me, and a lot better fiddler too. Remember the day when you said not to bring any dinner to school?"

"Ah-ha," Sandy nodded, one long finger up alongside his cheek. His voice was thin and Scotchy. "We come home and were rasping and scraping away at the fiddle when my father came in from the woods. He had his moggans on and there was lots of snow around. He'd been cutting wood."

"He saw us and wanted to know what we were up to and said for us to play a tune on the fiddle for him before he went out again. So we played something, and I scratched my way through. You remember what he said when we finished?"

"He said we'd never be fiddlers. Tooooo fast."

"Ah-h yes. That's what he said. Now, Jimmy Dubh," he said, turning to the old scholar, "this tune's for you."

Angus Allan played "Farewell to Loch Katrine" and Archie Neil carefully watched how Angus Allan held the bow at the tips of his thumb and one finger, his elbow doing the driving, and the fluid movements of his wrist. The music was sweet and light and strong as any he had ever heard.

"That's some scratchin'," said Ready Jack Comeau. "Now, there's one piece of yours I would like you to play. I play it on the harmonica, but I don't think I got it right." It was just a roundabout way of asking for "The Thunderbolt Reel."

Angus Allan complied at once, and while he drove her, the room shook with feet that could not be still. People had already found their way to the kitchen for a square set, half of them stepping away the entire figure. One old fellow who had done his drinking in preparation for the party was stepdancing, holding himself up against the wall. Angus Allan played a medley for the dancers, then he and Sandy MacLean played "Devil in the Kitchen" together, a tune filled with meticulous triple and double cuts.

"You know Dave Tom MacDonald," Rebecca Coady told Papa. She had a slow, gentle way of speaking. He nodded.

"Tom's boy," he said. "Over to Golden Grove. Married to the McDaniel girl—Maud, I think." Golden Grove was a huge farm across the river from the Chisholm farm.

"Well, there was square sets got goin' to our place, you remember, last July first, and Dave Tom asked me to dance with him. 'Ah, well, no,' says I, 'my back is hurtin' me pretty bad, and I haven't danced since awhile. Can't even get my work done lately.' But he was persistent, that boy, and he says, 'Oh, come on, Rebecca, dance with me anyways,' and I had to give in after awhile.

"Well, you know, as soon's he put his arm around my waist, that was it—the pain was gone. Like all at once. I danced and never felt a twinge. Should have thought of it myself, and asked him, him being the seventh son in that family."

Angus Allan came back into the main room. "You play a tune, Jimmy Dubh."

Archie Neil had been studying James D. Gillis. He had been told that Jimmy Dubh's parents died when he was young and that he was brought up by Angus Allan's grandfather, Hughie Gillis of South West Margaree. James D. was a strange looking man, severe and dignified. People said that he was a brilliant man, and a teacher; he had written books. He was wearing a ragged suit, very dirty, his shaggy white hair drooped from around his large, bald dome. His rubber boots were in the entryway and he now was wearing what once were socks, grimy feet showing through. He did not speak to Archie Neil, but when he spoke it was with precise enunciation, and an extremely courteous manner. He re-tuned a fiddle to scordatura—AEAE—and played two slow, beautiful tunes full of notes droning above and below the melody, which gave his fiddle music the thrum of a bagpipe. People stopped talking to listen to that old, old sound.

Some time past midnight, Momma forced Archie Neil to finally go upstairs. By the time he fell asleep at the top of the stairs, he had made up his mind to be a fiddler.

The party went on. Hector Smith broke in with a laugh. He told a story about how the devil chased him, nearly caught him, gave him such a scare he nearly cured him of drinking. And Momma laughed but told him he ought to tell the truth. So Hector said that she was absolutely right. "I'll tell you a true one. This happened up Foot Cape as well:

"There was a woman died and they were going through the woods, carrying her in the coffin. Two or three men, carrying her on their shoulders. And first thing you know, they hit a tree. And when they hit the tree, they thought they heard some noise inside. So, they put down the casket and they opened it up—it was only a homemade box you know—and, jeez, she was still alive.

"So they carried her back home. And, you know, she lived for about two years after that. Then, she died again.

"And they were going back, carrying the coffin, back along the same road through the woods. And the old man, her husband, he was coming along again in back of them.

"When they got near that tree, the old man in back hollered out, 'This time, boys, watch out for that tree!'"

Papa and Peter Pat roared and others laughed, but Hector's wife Flora had a dangerous look around her mouth.

"Clishmaclaver!" Momma said, quickly and sternly. It was her word for idle talk or blather. "It's better to stick with the truth. Now, this one is true, I heard it from my mother."

Momma settled herself in her chair and everyone waited. She could tell a good story. And she had the gift of mimicry.

"My grandfather was Rory MacLennan, and my grandmother Catherine MacFarlane, and you know that she was from South West Margaree. When she was a young girl just going out with Grandfather, there was a dance at her house. The weather was stormy, it was winter, and the fiddler didn't show up. And nobody had a fiddle or could do mouth music or anything like that.

"Now Grandmother was wishing so strongly for a fiddler, she said—and people heard her—'I wish some fiddler would come, even if it was Old Nick himself.'" Momma's voice suggest a coquettish young girl. "She was a good dancer, you see, and she wanted to impress Rory MacLennan.

"Well, okay. Nobody paid much attention. But in a little while there was a knock on the door and Catherine answered it. It was a stranger to her, a fine looking young man in a dark suit, with a fiddle under his arm.

"'I hear you are wanting a fiddler,' he said, and he took his cap off and bowed like Catherine was a great lady, the way he took her hand when he greeted her.

"'Who are you?' she asked him."

Then Momma's voice became manly but like silk. And there was a little bit of danger implied. She said, for the stranger, leaning in toward her listeners, "'I'm a Sasunnach, from over to Boston. I'm visiting relatives, and I got the message you might want a fiddler. Around here they call me Domhnull Dubh,' he said politely."

Momma leaned back and gave everyone time to focus on Black Donald.

"Catherine did not suspect who he was, and she had forgotten what she had said earlier. She thought he was called Black

Donald because he had very black, shiny hair. It did not strike her as strange that it was uncommonly long hair, neatly tied back with a black ribbon. His eyes were black, too, and they sparkled brightly when he looked at her."

Now everyone listening knew that it was a story. But they were all beyond true and untrue. They belonged to Momma, and to Black Donald as well. Momma shifted her voice and was Catherine again. A sweep of her arm and she told the other guests, "'Look, everybody. There's a fiddler here, name of Donald, and he'll play for us!'" Momma gathered her little circle closer. Across the room two fiddlers were playing "The Wedding Reels." Malcolm Post was pretending he'd sit by accident on a woman's lap, and "Away with you, you're awful" mixed with laughter.

"The guests were delighted to have a dance," Momma said, "and asked the fiddler if he could play this tune or that tune, all of their favourite tunes, and yes, he knew them, could play them all. He told them lots of Margaree-ers went to Boston over the years, and he had learned their tunes. He soon proved to be the best fiddler any of them had ever heard. He had tunes that they had never heard and his arm never tired and he played wicked variations and carried the medleys on and on, one tune so nicely fitting to the other. He was a delight. And they all danced and danced.

"And there was a little girl there. She was only five, the daughter of Dr. Angus MacLennan, Rory's brother. Some of you will remember him, they called him 'Le Gros Barb.'" Proud of MacLennan accomplishments, Momma added, "He's the one later went to Ottawa as an MLA.

"So, this little girl nudged her mother, and pointed to the fiddler, who was standing near the fireplace in the parlour.

"'What a funny foot he has,' she said.

"Her mother couldn't see, because of all the dancers on the floor. 'What is the foot like?' The little girl said, 'It is like a horses' hoof, only split.' She said it softly but everyone seemed to hear.

"The dancing stopped and the crowd cleared away for a moment, the mother still didn't see hoofs. She saw only patent leather shoes of two colours, with a fancy stitching coming down the centre and over the pointed toes. But she remembered the saying that the innocent can see things sinners cannot. And the fiddler kept playing and the dancers were taken up again in the wonderful music.

"But when Catherine came close, still dancing with Rory, the little girl's mother caught her arm and took her aside and told her. 'It is the devil you invited in to play the fiddle.'

"Catherine didn't believe her, but she was scared. She didn't want to take a chance. She spread the word to the dancers in the room by whispers, and the word got around, 'It's the devil playing the fiddle. The devil has all the best tunes.'

"The fiddler continued but the dancers stopped. They began to sing hymns. They sang so hard and loud it sounded like a Mass. They drowned the fiddler, and finally he stopped.

"Well, Black Donald looked spooked all right, at what was going on. Suddenly, there was a huge roar and a wind rose up outside and a loud crack of lightning. A tree fell close to the house, struck. Bushes were being torn up. The door blew open. The lamps went out, and all the smoke from the fireplace was pulled down the chimney and into the room. Och walie! they was all greetin' and snoolin', sure the end had come."

Momma was into the old dialect of her own Kintail Mac-Lennans. The story was telling the story.

"When the smoke cleared and they lit the lamps again, Black Donald was gone. All they found of him was three corbies' feathers." By which Momma meant they found the feathers of a raven.

"That was the lesson for Grandmother. Never to want anything so bad as to ask the devil for it. And she taught that to my mother. And my mother taught it to me."

Momma's spirit haunted the house the last weeks of that year. Christy had sent her money to visit her out West, the first time Momma had been anywhere since she was married. She went to see Christy and to meet Christy's husband, Frank Pillar, whose parents were immigrants from Germany. The house was not right without Momma any more than it was right when Papa was away. Willena had stopped her schooling that year to help out at home, and she was such a competent manager that

Momma left knowing that the household would run well. All of them, however, from Roddy to Angus thought Willena was excessively bossy, and let her know. But they appreciated her cooking.

Archie Neil shared in Momma's spirit with Willena, perhaps because the two of them were the ones most often home, and they both heard it: Momma's little cough. As if she were just in the next room, a kind of presence that they felt in the air, in the hair on the back of their necks, in glimpses of movement seen at the corner of the eye that disappeared when you looked that way directly. Both of them experienced it and said nothing to the other. And then one day, they were both in the kitchen, and they heard it at the same time coming from the living room.

Willena paused in her ironing. "Momma's here again today," she said to Archie Neil. "She's missing home."

"Yes, I heard it."

"What did you hear?"

"Momma's cough."

"That's what I heard too."

CHAPTER 8

Johnny Dan was a horse trader. He was an honest enough man, but horse trading to him was a sport. He once sold a neutered goat to a woman who hoped to raise goats. It did not bother him in the least; she should have known better. The same with horses. People often got the better horse from Johnny Dan. But when he traded a superior horse for one that was inferior, then he always had one eye busy looking around the stable, the kitchen, wherever they were dealing—looking for the "boot"—looking for that little sweetener to finalize the deal. It might be ten dollars thrown in "to keep us both honest." It might be a calf or a sheep, a set of tires. It might even be a date with somebody's daughter. One time it was a fiddle.

Johnny Dan appreciated music as a spectator sport.

This fiddle in particular looked like a good one, so he took it in a deal—the boot—then he carried it to Peter LeBlanc, a fiddler. Peter had traded a horse or two in his day. And he expressed doubt about the value of the fiddle. Was it worth fixing? Maybe the sound post could be set up a bit; maybe a new bridge was called for. The neck had definitely settled back. It would cost.

Actually, Peter liked that violin very much, and was delighted when Johnny Dan decided to leave it with him, "Do what you can with it." Two or three weeks went by and Peter did nothing but play that fiddle, and Johnny Dan wasn't claiming it. Peter started to think he owned the fiddle, one way or another. So he rigged it up properly to suit himself—a new bridge did the trick—and for him it was a sweet and responsive violin.

Now sometimes Willie D. Chisholm visited Peter LeBlanc, usually with a bottle. Willie D. was careful who he drank a-round. Momma was death on drinking. Papa took a drink but Momma rarely knew, and while he didn't want any of his children drinking, he tried to be realistic about it. Once when Roddy was caught, Papa had threatened him. But Roddy was twenty now, and sometimes he didn't bother to hide it from Papa. A kind of declaration of manhood. Papa said nothing to him, watched, but would not join him in a drink.

Willena and Mary Ann were nearly as adamant as Momma when it came to drink, and absolutely could not be counted upon to keep it secret if they smelled it on the brothers. So the boys were careful, and they'd cover for one another.

During one of Willie D.'s visits to Peter LeBlanc, they drank and sat quietly and Peter played the fiddle, just lovely slow airs. Then Johnny Dan came in, the first time since he'd left the fiddle. Willie offered him a drink, and for a time they all talked and joked about work and horses—and Peter just let the fiddle lay there. He didn't want Johnny Dan to know the fiddle was any good. But Willie D.—what did he know? He insisted Peter play the damn fiddle. Peter played, disgusted, and Willie D. and Johnny Dan drank.

After awhile, Johnny Dan told Willie he owned that fiddle and Peter told him that that was the truth. Then Johnny Dan said to Willie D., "I'll sell you that fiddle for $10.00." It was an awfully good buy and Willie D. wondered, Where was the boot? But Johnny Dan got ten dollars from Willie D. and all the boot he could hope for from poor, disappointed Peter LeBlanc.

Johnny Dan laughed loudly, slapping his thigh. He walked out still laughing. And Willie D. made Peter play that fiddle for him long after the bottle was empty. Then Willie D. took the fiddle home.

Through the night, Archie Neil and Angus heard Roddy and Willie D. arguing in a whisper, Roddy half-carrying him to bed. They giggled under the covers, knowing Willie D. was drunk, that the house was still peaceful, and that Willie D. was going to get away with it, again.

Angus grimaced. Archie Neil sawed at the fiddle. It was like when Mary Ann's boyfriend played and they were listening at the stovepipe. The fiddle squeaked. It rasped like a steel wire. It caterwauled. It squawked. It grated.

"Jeez," Angus said, holding his hands over his ears, in pain. "Here let me try it. You're not doing anything right."

He nestled the fiddle under his chin as he had seen other fiddlers. He held the bow delicately. He flexed his arm, adjusted his shoulders and the tilt of his chin, the angle of his wrist. Perfect. He touched the strings. They screeched in protest. He tried a different angle on the bow. The sound clawed the air, grinding upward to a whining pitch, punctuated by the sound of the kitchen door slamming.

They saw Papa through the window, retreating to the barn.

"Dhia!" Danny said, looking up from his book. "Why don't you try to play a tune?" Momma didn't complain. Being hard of hearing had advantages. All she had to do was go in another room.

It was weeks since the fiddle came. They had found it the next morning on the kitchen table. The crown jewels of England could not have astonished them more. There must be something wrong with the fiddle! But no, they knew the fiddle was fine because Peter LeBlanc visited one day and picked it up with a wistful sigh.

"Impossible for you two to learn." He sounded pretty sour. "No music in you at all."

To rub it in, he played a brief sweet tune.

Willie D. brought home some sheet music, but none in the family knew a note from a rabbit track.

"Let me try it again!" demanded Archie Neil. It was a recurring nightmare.

For a day or two, Archie Neil and Angus would both give up. People walked through the house with ease, not always ready to duck. And then the boys became possessed again.

"Maybe I'm holding it wrong."

Archie Neil held that instrument in an iron grip. Show it who is master. The music was in his head. He could hum it, he could sing it. Why couldn't he play it? He had tried being gentle with the fiddle; this time, it was going to play music or else!

But what came out of the elegant little fiddle was something like the death scream of a poorly slaughtered sow.

Then the bridge broke.

The quiet brought Papa back to the house. He saw the broken fiddle. "Sorry, boys," he said. "Too bad."

"We can get a new bridge for fifteen cents," Angus said. "Over to Doyle's store."

Papa put his hands deep into his pants pockets, and then patted the pocket on his shirt. "A little short right now." He couldn't stop smiling.

"Okay," said Angus. "Then I'll carve one."

It was a hot day in early August. The oats and barley were late this year because of a rainy July.

One of the chores Archie Neil was good at was making hay. He could handle the horse for cutting, and his powerful shoulders were just the thing for driving the lever forward on the hay rake. And as he raked hay, Archie Neil's mind was busy. He imagined himself a fiddler in the centre of a church picnic, everybody dancing to his music. He imagined getting invited to dances nearly every night and earning fists full of money. He was sought out to play at weddings and concerts, and was talked about, admired, especially by girls.

When he turned the horse, he could see Fordview across the river, Stephen White's place. That family was also busy with haymaking. Every one of Stephen's boys could play the violin. Johnny Stephen, for instance, had a solid instinct for the Scottish music and he could discern the slightest error in anyone's playing.

Yesterday, Archie Neil went with Papa to Stephen White's farm. While Poppa talked other business, Archie Neil talked with Johnny. It didn't take a lot of persuasion to get him to say that he would come to teach Archie Neil and Angus, get them started. Johnny was going off to look for work in Boston soon, and he said now was as good a time as any.

"If I ruin you, I won't be around to hear." Archie Neil's face turned to stone. Johnny Stephen told him not to worry. "I won't leave until either you're p-playing 'Cock o' the North,' or until Hell f-freezes over."

56

Johnny White said that that fiddle of Willie D.'s was in great trim. It had a new bridge, and all new strings. There was the steel E, and a catgut A and D. There was a gut-wound base, the G. This meant that running through the base string was a slender thread of catgut wound with wire to give it a heavier tone. Johnny explained all this, but Archie Neil was impatient to get to the music.

Right after lunch, the Chisholm family cleared out, and Archie Neil and Angus had Johnny Stephen all to themselves. He played "Cock of the North" for them, made them watch his fingers. He had his own fiddle and one of the boys had Willie D.'s. Johnny demonstrated how to correctly hold the fiddle and bow, and made each of them do it—"Don't want bad habits"— and then he showed them how to place the second finger and the index finger until, in theory, they should be able to play the first five notes of "Cock of the North," which he said was easy to play, a jig in 6/8 time with just two turns.

In two hours, sweat was pouring off of Johnny.

"I wish Hell would f-freeze over!" he said, rolling his eyes. He was a neat dresser, and now he looked as limp as his shirt. "Squeaks and h-howls!" he protested.

He consumed yet another cup of tea and approached them again like a foot soldier engaging the enemy, hand to hand. He would not give up, no—and those boys knew it. And despite the fear that he'd quit and leave immediately for Boston, Archie Neil thought, I'll never forget you did this, Johnny Stephen. Never. You are a hero.

In another two hours, Johnny had had several more cups of tea, and his shirt was ruined and he was a little worried about his heart. Archie Neil's fingers were sore, and his neck and wrist cramped. Angus, however, remained grimly absorbed, determined.

Then it happened: Angus played the five notes, a little raspy, but recognizable. Then Archie Neil did the same. A gleam of hope rekindled in Johnny's eyes. By late that night they learned enough notes to play the skeleton of their first tune. Angus got his first clear note.

Through it all, hardly noticed by the trio, the family had returned, eaten supper, gone back to the hayfield to work until dark, come back in, cleaned up and gone to bed, closing their doors firmly behind them.

Later that night, when Angus and Archie Neil were finally settled in their bed for the four hours left of night, Angus sat up. "Let's learn to play 'Father O'Flynn!'" He almost leaped out of bed to start at once. "It's a jig too."

"Shut up," Archie Neil said.

CHAPTER 9

With a few words and a last laugh, Mosie Coady, Peter Pat's son, left them close to the door, the horse and the wood sleigh swallowed up in the stinging snow and darkness.

Even in the quarter mile from Peter Pat's, where Archie Neil and Angus played for a dance, they were bitten by blustery December winds. They hurried into the kitchen entry, Angus out of his boots and into the warm kitchen. Archie Neil sat on the rickety chair in the cold room, thumped his crutches on the floor and reached down to tug off the rubber boots.

It was late and everybody was asleep. Papa had stoked up a good fire and the kitchen was warm. Angus investigated the cast iron pot on the counter and discovered about a quart of beans from supper. He dumped them in a frying pan, dug into a bag of onions and cut up two to fry with the beans. Soon the smell was heavenly, and despite the big meal they had at Peter Pat's, Archie Neil's stomach began to rumble. Neither boy could ever get enough food.

"I want some of those when they're ready," Archie Neil said, standing close to the stove, getting warmed.

Angus poured half of a jar of Momma's cucumber chow into the mix, and it smelled even better.

"Hell with you," he said, stirring the concoction and tasting a spoonful. "I want all of these. Get your own feed. There's some leftover turnip in the pan."

While the beans began to sizzle, Angus unwrapped the fid-

59

dle that Willie D. had bought, and he and Archie Neil shared. He was very particular about the fiddle, and he took it to their bedroom where it would be safe from the breakfast rush.

When Archie Neil listened to Angus play, he knew that Angus had a genius and passion for the violin that he lacked. He told himself that his own hands were hardened and his fingers were inflexible because of the use of the crutches; but he knew that that was not the reason he did not excel.

Archie Neil was satisfied that a few people were beginning to compliment him on his timing for the square sets; he prided himself on that reputation. It assured him of plenty of invitations to dances. Several local players had gone off to work in Vancouver and Boston and Detroit, meaning there were few players in the Margaree Forks area to play kitchen rackets and square sets. Archie Neil's passion was more for the invitations than for the fiddle. He liked being among people, having a good time. He was content to listen to Angus's long hours of practice while he read books or daydreamed.

He felt no resentment because Angus was a better fiddle player; but there were several pranks Angus had played on him recently, for which Archie Neil had come out badly. These rankled in his mind, especially after the incident today.

Francis Coady was their teacher, and he was very particular about English. One assignment was to look up every unfamiliar word. For homework the night before they had to read a poem which included the words "Sierras" and "minarets," both unfamiliar to Archie Neil.

Angus seemed to be getting ahead of him in learning meanings. They sat opposite each other at the kitchen table, trying to get the homework out of the way in a hurry. Last night Angus had the dictionary. There was also a long assignment ahead translating part of Virgil's *Aeneid* from Latin.

"Did you get the meaning of the words Sierras and minarets?" Archie Neil asked Angus.

"Yes," he said.

"Well, what do they mean?"

"Sierras are flat-roofed houses," Angus answered without missing a beat, "and a minaret is a slow dance, one-quarter time, I think."

The image seemed a little strained to Archie Neil, trying to envision flat-roofed houses dancing in one-quarter time, but sometimes poetry was like that, so he wrote it down. And the next morning he faced Francis Coady in English class. He felt good because he had his homework done. When it came to the word "Sierras," he put up his hand right away.

"Flat-roofed houses," he said.

Francis gave him a baleful glare.

"And minarets?"

"Slow dances," Archie Neil answered, "one-quarter time." He knew something was wrong even before the class laughed, and Archie Neil shot his brother with a bullet glare. He would pay for this.

"Flat-roofed houses, your grandmother!" Francis proceeded to lecture him about being more interested in fiddling than in his school work.

Angus was in great glee all day, but he gave Archie Neil a wide berth.

Now Angus cooked and refused to share, and Archie Neil worked on Angus's reward. Inspiration came when he glanced at the shelf where Momma kept a box of epsom salts. It was great for cleaning you out. It was also a golden opportunity. Quickly, he dumped about a quarter of it into the beans, mixing it in. When Angus came back to the stove, Archie Neil busied himself, putting another small stick in the firebox.

Then he sat across the table from Angus, eating turnips, watching Angus eat the beans.

After watching Angus slather five or six chunks of bread with butter, and brew up a pot of tea, Archie Neil went up to their bed, which was freezing cold. He snuggled down under the thick woolen blankets, feeling cosy, warm and filled with contented anticipation.

In awhile, Angus came to bed, and after a well-fed belch, poked Archie Neil with his elbow.

"That was some feed, boy. Sorry there wasn't enough for the two."

Archie Neil pretended to sleep, but within an hour a peculiar aroma began drifting around under the covers. He soon felt miserable. His trick seemed to turn against him; he could not

61

get far enough away from Angus without falling out of bed. And Angus slept.

Then he heard rumblings from Angus's stomach, like the approach of a geyser or of a train.

"Wonder what the hell is wrong with me," Angus said in the darkness.

Archie Neil kept up the pretense of sleep, and soon the distant train came closer, heading for the station. Suddenly Angus sprang out of bed.

As soon as he left the room, Archie Neil fanned open the bedcovers to let out the gas. Then he sat up against the headboard, his hands behind his head. He hummed a little jig that they had played at Peter Pat's. He could hear the kitchen door open, followed by the snarling of the dog, Snap, who resented being kicked from her place. Profanity drifted up the stairs, some of which he had never heard before. He visualized Angus pulling on the biggest boots he could find, perhaps taking time to pull on a coat over his longjohns, possibly not. Then Angus going around the barn and up the little hill to the outhouse. Then Angus finding that the door had blown open and the outhouse was half-filled with snow. The seat was icy. It was dark, the wind was howling, the snow beating in. Archie Neil loved it.

About ten or fifteen minutes later, Angus came back to the bedroom, his teeth chattering, which in no way interfered with the new dimensions of his vocabulary.

"Wonder what is wrong with me," he said again, truly perplexed.

"Hellish cold out there tonight, too," Archie Neil said, sympathetic, relinquishing his sprawl across the whole bed to avoid Angus's icy feet. "Bet the outhouse was half full of snow."

"More'n half of it. There's a drift, corner of the barn the whole way to the outhouse. Up to my waist.... Must be something I ate."

"Well, that cold meat at Peter Pat's tasted funny to me. You ate a half pound of it."

"Naw. You ate it too. Maybe them beans."

"Uh-uh. We have beans every week. Never bothered before."

Angus was about to say something else, but there were further rumblings. For ten minutes, he was silent, willing it to go away. He wasn't even warmed up yet. A branch of a tree scraped against the window. The wind was picking up, there was a swooshing of driven snow, a deepening cold seeping through the house. Archie Neil got up and added another blanket to the bed.

Angus muttered to himself; Archie Neil listened, picking up new words. Angus sprang from bed again and Archie Neil listened to Snap snarl at Angus as he crashed through the door, out into the dark. It was certainly not a minuet; it was more like a lively jig on the fiddle, played over and over that long night. Out of the Sierras went Angus, dancing the minaret.

CHAPTER 10

Some weeks later, Angus and Archie Neil arrived at Jimmy MacNeil's house on the Coady Road. Cassie MacNeil, his wife, was Papa's first cousin, and only because she requested it, Papa reluctantly allowed them to go.

It was a school night, and a sleety snow was falling, driven by wind from the west. Archie Neil was excited at the prospect of playing for the square sets tonight, for Jimmy and Cassie were very hospitable and they could be sure of a good feed and perhaps two dollars each at the end of it. Not only that, their kitchen rackets were always heavily attended.

Archie Neil had concealed that he was ill, fearing that he would be made to stay home and just Angus would get to go. There was a certain level of pain that never left him, but for several days now it was worse and he worried that somehow he had caught polio again. He kept these thoughts to himself; everyone at home was used to his moods. He felt tired and old, and the cold damp of the three-mile ride had not helped.

Angus was impatient and cold. After he had unhitched the horses and put them in the barn, Archie Neil was still in the wagon. He wanted to get in the warm house fast, but his legs were aching and leaden, and it was hard for him to move.

"What you waiting on?"

"You go on ahead," he answered. Angus took the fiddle and went in, while Archie Neil painfully climbed down and picked his way carefully over the few yards of icy snow to the door.

"Come in, Archie Neil," Cassie said, a big smile of welcome. He smiled broadly in return.

"Lovely summer evening," he said. "Hope it won't be too hot for the square sets."

She laughed, and Jimmy came over to shake his hand. "Glad to see you. Got a houseful tonight. They can't wait for the music! 'The Grey Goose.' Gawd, I love the way you play that tune."

"'The Grey Goose' it is," Archie Neil responded, cheerfully. Cassie took his coat and gave him a cup of hot tea, while in the living room Angus was already playing a tune and people were beginning to dance. Later, he would spell Angus. For now, he found a chair in a corner and tried to keep his aching legs from being bumped.

He played a few tunes after Angus, but he just couldn't seem to play with his usual vim. No one said anything, but more people danced when Angus played. Archie Neil sat again in the corner chair, next to the pantry. Shortly, he felt a hand on his shoulder. It was Ready Jack Comeau. "Come in here, Curly," he whispered. "I got something make you play that fiddle real good."

Puzzled, Archie Neil struggled up on his crutches and followed him into the dark pantry.

Ready Jack took out a flask. It was flat, slightly curved. He handed it to him. "St. Pierre special. The Real McCoy."

Archie Neil sipped it tentatively. It was a liquid inferno that travelled down his throat and into his stomach. He gasped and choked at the flash of fire. It was his first taste of liquor.

Jack was surprised. "You all right? You taste it before, eh?"

Archie Neil nodded. He wanted to appear a grown man in front of Ready Jack.

"I just swallowed it the wrong way," he said. "It's good." To prove it, he drank down two long, searing gulps.

Studiously, he pretended that it had no effect at all. "Thanks," he said. "The Real McCoy." However, the floor seemed to list upward in front of him for a moment, as if he were in a boat. He pretended that he knew it wasn't listing and walked out to the kitchen on a fairly even keel. When he sat, the chair seemed to tilt to the left, and he smiled at Ready Jack who was watching him with an amused grin. He pretended that the chair was steady. His chin and nose and lips were numb.

Cassie suddenly was in front of him and saying something, but her voice was hollow and he couldn't make it out. She was looking at him strangely. He concentrated. Yes, the sandwiches. He took two. After he ate them he felt better. Much better. His legs and back did not ache at all. His mind suddenly dropped its dark cloud of the past few days. He felt genial, exuberant, the equal of any or all.

He took more notice of the other guests. Most of them he knew well. Among them were three Campbell boys, and a Gillis he knew from school, and they all had girlfriends, most of whom were also from the Forks, or nearby schools. But there was one girl he had seen once or twice, heard about, but did not know. She came from a well-to do family in Sommerville, near Boston, was out of school, visiting her LeBlanc relatives. She was perhaps three or four years older than he was, and looked different from the Forks girls. Her dark hair was cut in a short bob that hugged her head in sculpted waves; she wore a straight mauve dress of some knitted fabric that was cut with no waistline but with a wide band of silk around the hips—a relaxed, elegant look, he thought, which suited her well. He noted that she wore stylish shoes and probably silk stockings.

He went into the living room when she did, and watched her dance in the sets, full of exuberance. He fell in love with her then, but even more so when she seized the opportunity between sets and sang to her own piano playing. The younger guests soon gathered around and sang with her. She played "Yes, We Have No Bananas" and "Ukulele Lady" and "Yes

Sir, She's My Baby." She had a racy strong voice, full of man-
nerisms and stylings unfamiliar to the older people. She also
played for two of her friends who wanted to demonstrate something called The Charleston. The older people were polite, but
Archie Neil knew they were shocked, or baffled. It seemed a
little indecent. What good was jazz for square sets?

Ready Jack Comeau sat down near him. "How you feeling,
Archie Neil?" He followed Archie Neil's gaze to the girl.
"Great party, eh?"

"Yeah," Archie Neil said. "What is her name?"

"Katie Burns." Then he added, "It's almost as good as Basil's wake," as Katie Burns went up the stairs with some other
girls, and out of sight.

Ready Jack laughed. "I met my wife at Basil's wake. Back
then she was petite bouette"—the Chéticamp word for bait used
to catch cod. "Just like that little Katie. Nice leg on her."

Basil's wake, some twenty years before, was legendary, the
best attended and most enjoyed wake in the history of Margaree Forks. It was the finest session of gossip the neighbours had
experienced all that winter; the liquor flowed, the fiddle never
stopped, two new courtships were struck up, and everyone was
late for the funeral the next day. While the deceased would
have enjoyed these proceedings as much as anyone there, the
priest was scandalized.

"Well, there is a good story about another wake," Ready Jack
said, tipping his chair back against the wall and lighting a cigarette with the air of one utterly content. Paddy Gillis, nearby,
took this as a signal to listen more carefully, and so did several
others. Ready Jack did have good stories in him.

"This widow, Mabel, live with her mother and the old mother
die. They don't have much, just a cabin—not much in it. Three
sons of Mabel come from away to pay respect. She make them
busy, cleaning, cooking, making the casket before the wake, you
know. She say to one son, 'Alex, go get material for a shroud, and
get two packages icing sugar in Inverness.' Alex, he was glad to
go to Inverness. He have on his mind a little rum cheer-up.

"Meanwhile Mabel, she get nervous waiting. She say to the
second son, 'That no good Alex is drinking, I know it. Billy,

you go to Inverness. Get material for the shroud. And don't forget two box of icing sugar.'

"But the store is near a tavern and Billy went in for just one little drink. By this time, it is late, mind you, and the old mother is laid out on a door on two sawhorse without a shroud. So Mabel sends Dan Joe for the cloth and for the icing sugar, and he look in the store at this cloth and that cloth but can't make up his mind. So he joins Billy at the tavern, for one drink. Mabel is upset when he don't come back neither.

"Now Red Ranald MacDonnell, he came to Mabel's door. My God, he feel sorry for poor Mabel.... You know him, eh? A fine fellow. Never miss a wake, or a wedding in fifty year—he like a good time, Red Rannie.

"He saw the boys come in the house one after the other. Each one got two box icing sugar. Now Mabel is some mad, eh? 'What in the name of God I gonna do with six boxes of icing sugar, and no shroud?' Ranald say to her, 'Now Mabel, calm yourself. Make do with what you have.' He didn't want her to feel bad. She throw her hands up to Heaven. 'Ranald, I don't have a thing to use, not a thing. What am I gonna put on me mother?'

"Ranald said, 'If you don't have a shroud, then just frost her.'"

Paddy Gillis and the other listeners had a good laugh over that. But while Ready Jack had been talking, Archie Neil not only listened but was also trying to think of a story he could tell that everybody had not yet heard. Before Ready Jack's last line, he had already settled on the story, the opening line (from Papa's style of telling a story), and several embellishments of his own.

After a few moments, and before anyone else could start a story, Archie Neil said, "I read in the newspaper Sandy MacAlpine passed away. Poor fellow. Only married two years."

This drew blank expressions. They never heard of Sandy MacAlpine.

"From Inverness," Archie Neil said. "No older than you, Jimmy." He wagged his head in sorrow.

"What about him?" asked Jimmy MacNeil.

"It started years ago," said Archie Neil. "He courted two girls, Maggie from Inverness Marsh, and Sara from Foot Cape.

Neither one of the girls knew about the other, even though he had been seeing them both for eight years. As far as he was concerned, it was like eating his cake and having it. Having two girlfriends gave zest to his life. They cooked nice things when he visited. They treated him like royalty.

"He liked both the girls so much that he couldn't make up his mind between them. Maggie was blonde, good build on her, and could turn heads no matter where she was. A great dancer too, the life of a party. Sara was dark-haired and pretty, but quieter. She had a good sense of humour and worked hard. Everybody loved Sara once they got to know her.

"One day Sandy's mother got mad at him for dragging on this way."

Archie Neil changed his voice to the mother's. "'Sandy, this is not fit. You are committing mortal sins with these two girls. Ruining their lives.'

"'All right,' Sandy said. 'I'll tell you what I'll do. I will hitch up the buggy tonight, and tie the reins around the whip handle. I will start the horse.' "

Archie Neil paused, and looked around at several people who were listening. "I don't want to bore you," he said.

"Archie Neil," Ready Jack said severely, "you don't finish this story, you never get home tonight. So shut up and talk."

"'I will start the horse at the lane,'" Archie Neil resumed, in the voice and manner he had given to the character of poor Sandy MacAlpine. He loved the attention. "'If the horse turns right and goes to Sara's place, I'll propose to her. If he goes left to Maggie's place, I'll propose to her.'

"The horse went left. Sandy got out of the buggy with his hat in his hand and knocked on Maggie's door. When she answered, he said, 'Maggie, I have come to ask you to marry me.'

"'Sandy, it's about time.'" Archie Neil gave Maggie's voice a sharp edge. 'We've been going together for eight years. You should know me by now.'

"'Well then,' he said, 'we'll have the banns published next Sunday.'

"Hearing the banns this way gave the poor Sara much hurt and sorrow. She was a sweet creature who really loved him. However, there were no lack of other fish in the sea, and before another year passed she was married. She was an excellent wife, and her husband was happy and prosperous.

"Sandy and Maggie also got married. But it seems he didn't know her at all. She had a desperate temper. From the first day of marriage, she bossed him. 'This is what you get for making me wait for eight years, Sandy MacAlpine,' she said. Sandy was quickly getting old before his time, his heart was going bad on him. He figured he would be the first man in history to die from a nagging wife. All he could think about was that horrible day he let the horse choose his fate.

"He got no sympathy from his mother, either. 'You'd think a man would have more sense than a horse,' she said when he complained."

Archie Neil paused again. He took a leisurely sip of tea. Ate a bite of oatcake.

"Well? What happened?"

Archie Neil kept himself from grinning. He put on a serious face. Thought: one, two, three. Then said:

"He shot the horse."

Archie Neil felt that he had never yet played the fiddle as well as he did that night, especially after Ready Jack took him on another trip to the pantry. This time Angus went too and had his first drink. While Archie Neil played after that, it seemed to him that Katie Burns cast flirtatious looks in his direction. The music sprang from his fingers so that people shouted, "Let 'er rip, Archie Neil!" and demanded tune after tune. It didn't seem to bother them that he had a limited repertoire. He played "The Grey Goose" three times.

He felt confident; he joked and laughed and had the best time of his life. He even talked briefly to Kate. She would be spending the summer at her uncle's house and she would play piano for him since he liked jazz tunes so well.

About 2 a.m., just as Archie Neil and Angus were leaving, Wilfred McDaniel stopped them at the doorway. He was an assistant to Francis Coady at the Margaree Forks school. "You two are getting so good," he said, "I want to ask you something. My brother, Peter Mose, is getting married. Suppose you can play for the wedding?"

Archie Neil's heart leaped. It would be their first wedding! He wanted to say yes instantly, but he had to be careful. "Thanks," he said. "We'll have to see what our father says. I think it will be all right."

When they left the yard in the wagon, the brothers whooped for joy.

The cold was exhilarating, their pulses raced, the snow coming down danced before the fiddlers. Giggling and holding one another up, they somehow got up the stairs and into their bedroom, falling asleep happy and fully clothed.

The next morning was horrible. The ache in his legs had returned with a vengeance; his head ached; he was sure he was going to throw up. Angus looked crumpled and cross. But both of them went to school and said nothing.

CHAPTER 11

The rhythm of Margaree River life has its human counter-pulse. At breakfast one Saturday in early June, Papa announced that he was tired of corned beef and beans. For supper there was to be a feast of salmon. Archie Neil rode in the wagon with Papa, down to the Forks Pool. He was not able to fish, but he enjoyed the sights, sound, and smell of the river, and a rare opportunity to be alone with Papa.

They said little. Archie Neil was immersed in Robert Burns, poems about Mary asleep by a murmuring stream, false loves, streams around the castle of Montgomery, and the loss of his sweet Highland Mary. Papa was busy with his own thoughts. But it was a companionable and comfortable silence they shared.

Archie Neil was well hooked on stories and tunes, even if he had never hooked a fish. He was deliberately building up a repertoire of both—and people had started looking forward to what he had to offer, especially his stories.

Otherwise, he remained the spectator. The sight of boys heading down for swimming still evoked envy. They all went. But not him. They went to a swimming hole near an old narrow, partly covered bridge. They stood on the third rail and dove into the river. Angus described it in detail. Sometimes they went to a pool at East Margaree where the water was very deep. The thought of diving into the radiant amber water, of the exuberance of the splash, of cool deep effortless sliding like a salmon, of sunburned laughter—all this was a bitter picture, forever out of his reach. Perhaps if he had been one of them, it would seem commonplace, soon forgotten. But he was never one of them, and though he thought of himself as virtually a man now, there was still a boy in him, standing on the veranda watching them head for the river, leaving him behind.

The same was true of salmon fishing. It was not the sport of it so much as the vision of himself landing a fish and presenting it for his mother's table, winning everyone's admiration. But his legs could not hold him in the current, or brace him against the pull of a fish on his line.

Archie Neil twiddled with the pencil nervously. He was not sure that he would pass the Provincial Examinations. Every year some students failed, after waiting six weeks for the grades. A crown left on the top of the paper meant passing; if it was torn off, failure. And that meant another year in the same grade, and taking the exams over again. If a student failed one subject, he failed everything. This morning was geometry, this afternoon trig—each exam two and a half hours long. There were seven more exams that week.

Archie Neil knew he hadn't studied enough, spending a lot of school time on pranks and socializing, then hasty homework before a night of fiddling. His grades were just high enough to avoid conflict with Momma and Papa. But Provincials were the true test. No charm, no sympathy, no power of persuasion, and no excuses.

There were about fifty students in the room on this hot Monday in the last week of June. They came to Margaree Forks from Belle Côte and North East Margaree, Big Intervale, Portree, Cranton Section and Gillisdale. Norry Chiasson, a blacksmith and former teacher, was the examiner, and there were two monitors, men of the right political party. This was a plum of a job—a week's work at $5.00 a day.

Grade 11 was the highest in these schools. Archie Neil was assigned a number and a seat, and sat stiffly, keeping his eyes forward, as they passed out the envelope with the questions. The envelope had three seals. Norry went around the room, opened each envelope, and placed the question sheets face down so that all the students would begin at the same time.

Norry looked at the pads of foolscap each student carried in, gave a cursory glance at magazines students were allowed to bring to use as a writing pad between the foolscap and the hard desk. Archie Neil was very conscious that any wrong move could result in being accused of copying or cribbing.

Janet Morris sat to one side of Archie Neil. She wore a big picture hat with a wide brim—to take an exam, he thought.

Archie Neil was good at geometry, but he decided to take his time, unlike some others who wanted to get done, get out and be free of it.

It was not long before a subtle movement on his right attracted his attention. Janet was bent down writing, the brim of her hat coming to the edge of the desk. Her eyes were busy looking at the monitors, and every once in a while turning a page of her magazine. Archie Neil saw that she had written theorems and proofs on pages of the magazine. Janet was about the best-dressed and prettiest girl at the Forks, and she was supposed to be one of the smartest. She never had much to do with him, but that did not prevent him from admiring her. Now, his estimation plummeted.

He wanted to laugh and he wanted to trip her up, get her discovered. He caught her glance just long enough to let her know that he knew what she was doing. In a few minutes he raised his hand. Janet froze in turning a page. He asked to go to the bathroom, and as he got up with his crutches, he pretended to slip and his crutch almost knocked her magazine to the floor. Hastily, she caught it. He was escorted out by one of the monitors. He knew she would be wondering if he would tell.

When he returned, she gripped her foolscap and magazine grimly, casting him a look of mixed hatred and appeal. He kept his face blank. The monitor made two or three passes in their direction. Once, when the monitor was on the other side of the room and Janet was turning a page, Archie Neil raised his hand to ask for a fresh pencil. After that Janet didn't dare turn a page.

The night Archie Neil got his Provincial Exams back, a crown at the top and respectable marks, he played fiddle at a dance. He stood tall, proud. Getting Grade 11 was a feat that many people at the Forks had never accomplished—even a number of the teachers! He thought of himself as accomplished, but he decided to appear modest.

Papa was already talking about Archie Neil and St. Francis Xavier University in perhaps a year or two. If he were able to find the money. If he could find transportation. If Archie Neil was able to climb the stairs and get to the classes. Solutions seemed improbable to Archie Neil. However, just discussing the possibility pumped up his self-esteem.

He felt like a little crowing that night, and made outrageous remarks to the girls that made them laugh, and told off-colour stories to the other fiddlers that made them sputter into their drinks. The host was generous with drinks for the fiddlers, and Archie Neil felt in rare good form. He was, in fact, bordering on being drunk. Janet was among those at the dance. He had heard that she flunked geometry.

"You know, on the geometry exam, did you get that question about the Pythagorean Theorem?" he asked her during a break in the dancing. Even to his own ears, he sounded pompous and smug.

"I don't remember," she said with a withering look. "I thought it had to do with a bag of hot air—a blimp, or was it a gimp?" She turned her back on him, and then turned to him suddenly. She said, "Heard somebody say that they found crib notes in the bathroom."

Janet said something to her companions, loud enough for him to hear, about going to another dance where the fiddler wasn't a show-off rummy.

CHAPTER 12

Paved roads were the rarity. There were none in the area of the Margarees. The roads were dirt—mud in spring—or gravel. The few who had cars in 1925 used them only in the summer and fall, then put them on blocks, took off the tires for the winter. Sleighs or wagons carried them through those months. Still, even having a car in the barn was a thing of status, a symbol of worldly success.

Alex Jim McDaniel inherited a small grocery store from his father, a short distance down the road from the Chisholm home. He kept it well-stocked and he had prospered. Alex Jim decided to branch out, bought a 1923 Ford, and travelled the district buying lambs in the fall. He came back with the car heaped with a pile of trussed lambs, which Roddy Chisholm butchered. Then Alex Jim marketed them in Sydney, picking a cool day for the eight-hour drive on the twisty, rough roads.

Archie Neil was often idle that long summer, reading on the veranda or taking short walks on crutches. Sometimes Alex Jim roared by, braked the car with a screech and a cloud of dust, ground into reverse and told Archie Neil to jump in. Archie Neil was delighted; he didn't care where they were going.

Alex Jim was a man no one could lean on. He had a good enough heart when he was sure he was helping someone who needed it, but he could turn around on a whim. Archie Neil had seen him blow up at a customer in the middle of the sale, shoo everyone out of the store, and lock up for the day.

Alex stopped the car in the middle of the road. Got out and came around to Archie Neil.

"Get over there and drive that car," he ordered. He opened the door, pushed Archie Neil behind the steering wheel, and took the passenger seat.

Archie Neil sat there puzzled. His heart pounded and his palms were wet. He had never driven a car. He bent forward and studied the dashboard, then quickly sat upright, like a chauffeur. Alex bit off a chunk of tobacco and chewed furiously. Archie Neil knew something about cars. He had looked into cars parked at the river while tourists fished a pool. And he had read about cars.

There were the three little pedals. Under the left foot was the clutch, and when you pressed it in you put the car in low gear. In the centre was the pedal for reverse. The right foot pedal was for the brake. The emergency was near the left hand. It was not just a brake, it was the only way to put the car in neutral. When the emergency was vertical, the car was in neutral. The gas and the spark were up under the steering wheel. Archie Neil ran his hands over the wheel. This was beginning to feel good. He had watched when Alex drove.

"Well, what you waiting on?" Alex said. "Drive!" A spit and more chewing.

Archie Neil started the spark, pulled down the gas, pressed the starter, pulled down the spark, and eased up on the gas. He forgot to put his foot down on the low gear pedal, and the car started with a violent jerk and stalled. "Huh!" Alex said, but he offered no advice. Archie Neil tried again, realizing that he had to get sufficient speed in low gear before releasing the clutch and letting the engine slip into high. The car jerked and stalled at each attempt.

His heart fell. He was embarrassed. But more important, he didn't want to lose this chance. Alex could just as well leap out of the car and shut down for the day. But finally Archie Neil had to say, "I can't do it. I don't have enough in my legs to push the pedals."

Alex spit. "You can do it if you want to," he said. "Don't give yourself so many excuses. You got to learn sometime. Now's as good a time as any. Drive."

Archie Neil tried again, and got the motor running. He found that he could handle the steering wheel and gas lever with one hand. With the other hand, he pressed down on his knee, giving that leg enough force to put the Ford in low gear. With his heart in his throat, Archie Neil drove about fifteen yards, narrowly missed a hitching rail and a sleeping dog.

Then he panicked and hit the brake and the car stopped and stalled.

"Jumpin' Jesus," Alex Jim said. "You wreck this car, and I'll use that crutch over your head." Then softly, steadily: "Give it more gas, you damn fool."

Alex Jim had him driving up and down the road for two solid hours, the road virtually to themselves.

At the end of it Archie Neil was shaky with exhaustion and exhilaration. He could drive a car!

"Alex, I don't know how to thank you," he said, as he got out in front of his own house.

"You just be ready to drive when I need a driver," he responded. With no more adieu, he turned the car and zoomed away.

At the railway station in Inverness, Momma, Papa, and Archie Neil said good-bye to Willie D., who was taking the Judique Flyer to meet the Harvest Excursion train bound for the prairies.

The summer before, Mary Ann was also swallowed by the train; she was now in Weyburn, Saskatchewan, teaching. Her letters told of discontent with the poor pay for teachers, and of her resolve to earn enough money to go to Boston to study nursing.

Archie Neil felt as though life was coming apart. Now Jack, Christy, Mary Ann, and Willie D. were gone. Danny was eager to leave. Willena was planning to marry Mike Murphy. Angus was restless, discontented, more distant than he used to be.

Roddy was an anchor, with no desire to see the world, only to conquer his own. Roddy worked in the woods from May to late fall, spent a month or so at home, and then went back to the Highlands to haul out pulp. In the spring he'd follow the drive down North River or load pulp on board a ship in St. Ann's Bay. Months passed when they seldom saw him. He lived his own life. With plenty of young women interested in him, he had not found the one he wanted to marry.

The night of Willie D.'s departure, Archie Neil had a nightmare. He was standing on the bank of the Margaree. He looked down and was surprised to see that he was no longer crippled, but was whole and strong. There was a fallen log across the river, and on the other bank were clouds of smoke or steam. He felt compelled to walk across the log to where Willie D. and Jack and Christy and Mary Ann were waiting for him. Then Janet Morris shouted. "I know you! You think you're so great, but I know the truth!" Then she jumped on one end of the log and knocked him off into the water, and he fell very, very slowly, a long way down. The water was roaring. All around him in the water were salmon. He could not see them, but felt their presence. He was a salmon too. The current wasn't pulling him, and ahead was a definite place he was going, but he could not see it and he could not find the way. He just knew it was there and finding it or not finding it was life or death. He was gliding, and whether the river was taking him or he was a swimmer he did not know, but he was in the water sweeping over the same round smooth stones of the riverbed, over and over again. Then something was suspended in the water, enticing. It was beautiful; it fascinated him. He took it in his mouth and it pierced him. He fought it desperately, but became tired and was pulled up onto the bank, into the drowning air....

Angus shook him awake. He had been thrashing wildly in his sleep.

CHAPTER 13

Archie Neil dozed on the wagon seat at the Gordon farm. He had agreed to drive home two friends who were helping with the hay and they had just left for the last load. It was a windy evening; the rustling of drying leaves mixed with the hum of insects and birdsong. Everything made the late afternoon seem sensual to him, even the dryness made him think of warm rain. And of Kate.

She was visiting from Sommerville; he had seen her two days ago outside her uncle's house. Archie Neil and Angus were loading shingles for Papa's new barn. Kate was sitting on the front steps and he could hear her laughter. She noticed him and waved, and Archie Neil made an excuse to stay while Angus shifted the box cart and unloaded. He joined her on the step and they talked about nothing, but he made her laugh, and he loved her eyes. She seemed to think he was charming, witty. He feasted on this. He tried to be even more charming, more witty. He was sure she gave him signals, a slight touch, that it was all right, don't try so hard. By the time Angus returned with the cart, yes, she thought it would be fun for them to see each other this summer. She would be at the dances. She leaned a second against him. He almost kissed her. But he was chicken.

That Sunday, he watched Kate Burns in church. She sat with her cousin Una. He had learned a new word from Robert Burns: "sonsie." Yes, she was sonsie. Sweet, sonsie Kate. He wondered if Kate were related to Robert Burns, way back. He thought about kissing her. He knew Robert Burns would not have been afraid.

Dougald MacKenzie slid into the pew next to Archie Neil. "Nice view," Dougald whispered.

The congregation stood when Father Cormier entered from the sacristy with two altar boys. Then just before the Gospel reading, Willy Fisher slid into the pew in front of Dougald and Archie Neil, and Kate had to move further down. Willy was a poor substitute. He took off his hat. It left his bald head encircled with a halo of newspaper. Willy had inserted the strip of newspaper inside the crown to make the hat fit. It usually stayed inside the hat. Dougald's eyes asked Archie Neil which of them was going to tell Willy Fisher.

"Wait," Archie Neil whispered. "I want to read the headlines."

He caught a look from Father Cormier. Archie Neil did not want trouble. Father Cormier was death on dances, and Archie Neil had helped start a weekly dance, open only to singles under thirty. They were ready for Father Cormier to raise the roof over it. Archie Neil figured they had it over him on a technicality. The hall was in South West Margaree, just out of Father Cormier's precincts, so to speak. So far, the good father had not said a word about the dances. And he didn't want to draw his attention.

"I am carnal, sold under sin." Father Cormier seemed to speak to Archie Neil. He quoted St. Bernard, that thought becomes an impure flame that drags the soul to eternal punishment. "Impurity is a viper whose head must be crushed," he said, "for it is mortal sin and a poison."

Archie Neil looked at the statue of the Virgin Mary, her foot on the head of a snake. He felt a little ashamed. He tried not to look again at Kate. But the flame was not easily doused. Sweet, sonsie Kate. The words involuntarily returned, and the stirrings in him as well. He worried about going to communion, whether he was already guilty of a mortal sin....

After church Alex Jim McDaniel singled out Archie Neil. "Look, tomorrow I'm doing a sheep drive down to Nyanza," he said. "Stayin' overnight in Sydney. Now don't you tell me you're too busy to come and get me on Tuesday with the car. I'll be coming off the *Blue Hill* at Nyanza about one o'clock. Bloody well be there." He stomped off as if Archie Neil had offered nothing but grief and arguments. He turned a few yards away, and said, "And I suppose you'll have to get the car Monday night. You can pick it up at six. Not one minute earlier."

Archie Neil stood, dumbfounded. Driving to Nyanza! Having the car Monday night! Katie was just riding off with her uncle and aunt and cousins in their rig, and he hobbled towards them faster than he had ever moved in his life, but they were still too fast.

"Kate!" he shouted. The uncle reined the horse in, and Archie Neil caught up to them. He was nervous, excited. But he didn't think about who heard him or saw his rough run on crutches.

"Kate," he said. "How would you like to go for a drive tomorrow night? In a Ford! At six." The cousins giggled; he ignored them.

"I'd love to," Kate said, as the uncle, disgusted, started the horse away. "I'll bring a picnic supper!" she shouted back.

At the little log school opposite the Margaree church, Archie Neil and Freddy LeBlanc played on Saturday night. To make room for the dancers, he and the young mandolin player sat on chairs on top of a table. At times, a fiddler from Chéticamp shared the table with them, and Freddy was beside himself with the worry both that the table would collapse and that he couldn't get Archie Neil and the other fiddler, on either side of him, to play the same tune, at least the same beat. Freddy was a great admirer of Archie Neil who taught him tunes and had gotten him started playing mandolin at dances. It turned out to be a popular combination and they often played together with great success. "We'll make those dance tunes sing," Archie Neil often said to him. And, generally, it was true. But not this dance.

"I can't play with you fellows. You're not together."

"Just play hard on the A and E," Archie Neil advised him. "We'll stick to the easy drunken tunes."

Freddy looked around at the dancers. Drunken tunes matched the crowd. "This table will give out for sure."

Archie Neil patted his bottle. He had thrown away the cap. "If it does, I'll grab the life preserver, Captain." Freddy was not reassured.

Archie Neil took another swig of the bottle, and offered up a toast to the rowdies on the dance floor. "Here's to William the Third and Anne Boleyn!"

The dance turned out to be just the kind that Father Cormier condemned. Charlie Ivy was being chivvied by a group of fellows from St. Rose who were bad buggers when they were drinking, spoiling for a brawl. Soon dancers were swinging to their own tune, Archie Neil playing on with a merry jig, stopping to push an occasional fighter away with his crutch. He saw Charlie Ivy duck out the front door, running as if demons were after him. And when the fight broke out, a St. Rose boy crashed against the back door that was never used. It opened and he disappeared with a flash of surprise across his face. The bank at the back of the school dropped off at least 15 feet. He was swallowed and heard of no more that night.

It was too good to be true. Archie Neil took an extra bath Monday morning, which meant again dragging out the galvanized tub and monopolizing the kitchen, kettles and pans collected on the hot stove. Willena and Momma were cross because it was a laundry day and the house would be even hotter in the afternoon. He pestered Willena to press his shirt. He borrowed Roddy's suit jacket, despite Roddy was fifty pounds heavier, and taller. The coat was a fine light grey, a colour in which Archie Neil looked good. He borrowed a straw hat from Angus.

He spent an hour in front of the old leprous mirror shaving and then trying to Brilliantine the curls out of his hair. It was one battle he lost. He used Roddy's aftershave, Taylor's Lilas de France. In the end, he thought he cut a fine figure of manhood.

As he was leaving to see Kate, he passed Peter Pat's gift of tiny crutches hanging in the entry shed. He outgrew them but kept them. He wished that his present pair were hanging beside them. But every attempt to walk without crutches had failed. The left leg had strength for standing, but it was like a broken hinge when he tried to walk. He had to press his hand against his left knee to keep it from buckling. To hell with that. He was driving a car, wearing a straw hat, and having a picnic with Kate. When he sat behind the wheel, he was sure he had never been happier in his life.

Archie Neil spent one of his three dollars on gas. Twenty-five cents on a bottle of moonshine. Kate had hinted that she might take a little nip. After his grand arrival at Kate's uncle's, he demonstrated his driving prowess. He looped the road to the North East, went to Margaree Harbour, and took the high road across the river as far as Tom MacDonald's. From there they took a wagon road down to Golden Grove, and had their picnic under an elm tree near the river.

Kate had brought roasted chicken, fresh buttered bread, a thermos of hot tea, and pie for dessert. She spread it out on a tartan blanket, and was so careful and precise about how things looked on their dishes that Archie Neil was totally charmed. She even sipped the moonshine elegantly, from a teacup. She was a bright little minx, he thought. "Minx" was another new book word.

"Your Father Cormier really does impose impossible standards. He makes sinners and hypocrites out of all of you."

Archie Neil had not considered it that way. It was hard to turn that into a joke.

"Now, our priest in Sommerville, he's more enlightened. He doesn't try to make us guilty about not being perfect. He talks to us gently and reasonably. Encourages us to do better."

"There are some of us saints, though," he said. "You were sitting next to one in church. You saw Willy Fisher's halo."

Kate laughed and threw church to the wind.

"It's beautiful here," she said dreamily. They had packed up the picnic things and were leaning against the car. He imagined she must be a little chilled in the evening air, and so he put his arm around her shoulders, and she didn't mind. She wore a white dress with a print of lilac sprigs, and to him there had never been a more beautiful creature.

The sun was slanting across the fields. A thin mist rose from the river, and there was just enough breeze to keep away mosquitoes and black flies.

"I've often thought I'd like to live at the Forks," she said. She pulled away from him to smooth her hair, the small act somehow suggesting that living at Margaree Forks was out of the question. "But women really have it rotten here. They work so hard for so little. Such narrow lives. Women live better in Sommerville."

Archie Neil pretended to take offense. "We think Boston girls are uppity and citified. Putting on airs is a mortal sin here, you know."

"I know." She laughed. "But you are all backwards. And that's not all bad, you know. In some ways, it's nice. Actually, there are people here I like a whole lot." She looked right at him.

"Well, I think people from Boston are backwards."

"Oh?" Now she feigned offense.

"There was a fella from Boston, not long ago, fishing this very spot of the river," he said. "Only it had been a dry summer. You could almost walk across the river. And he told my friend Duncan MacKenzie that the day before, he caught a 26-pound salmon in this pool."

"So? A lot of people do that."

"Not that summer. The river was pretty well empty of salmon. Low water, and warm. 'Well, my dear man,' this fella was saying—and in a good rich Boston accent—'peculiar things can happen in this river.'"

Archie Neil changed his voice to Duncan's. "'Yes, strange things happen in the river. I can remember last year,' said Duncan, 'and in this very spot too, I latched on to a huge big salmon. And when I reeled it in, it had a lantern in its mouth. And that lantern,' Duncan told him, 'was lit.'"

"Come on," said Kate, "the lantern wasn't lit."

"That's just what the Boston fella said. And in a voice something like yours: 'Come on, Duncan. That's impossible. The lantern wasn't lit.'"

"So what did Duncan say?"

Archie Neil put on his best Duncan voice. "'Okay,' he said. 'If you'll take ten pounds off your salmon, then I'll blow out the lantern.'"

Kate punched his arm, but she had to laugh. "I'm always laughing when I'm with you," she said. "I like that."

"But oh, I'm a desperate serious fellow, Kate," he said. "I mean to kiss you before I take you home."

"You'll have to catch me first!" she said. She kicked off her shoes and ran to the edge of the river and gathered her skirt above her knees and waded in. Recent rains had made the river swift, but she had no difficulty.

"Come in. The water is warm and beautiful," she said.

"I can't," he said, beginning to lose his humour.

"Yes, you can. Come on. If you do—who knows what strange things are happening in this river!" She looked very pretty, framed by the sky in the river.

"I'll fall."

"So what? You won't drown."

"Yes, I will."

"I'll save you," she countered. He could see her face, and he could see neither pity nor ridicule.

He hobbled over the uneven ground, down to the river edge. She came forward as if to help, then she splashed him mercilessly.

"I'll get you for this."

"Please do." She waded out of the water and kissed him right on the mouth.

It was getting dark now, and they returned to the car.

CHAPTER 14

By ten the next morning, Archie Neil was dressed in his best clothes and off on his thirty-mile trek to Nyanza, his first trip over that particular road in any vehicle. Fifteen miles an hour was a reckless speed most of the way, the crookedest and narrowest road he had ever seen. In places near Lake O'Law, alder branches scraped both sides of the car, and there were deep ruts to thud through and the occasional little wash-out. At the approach to Hunter's Mountain, Archie Neil began to have serious doubts about continuing, sorry he had his suit coat on, his shirt wet with sweat. But the thought of Alex Jim waiting forever on the wharf in Nyanza was incentive enough. Besides, he couldn't turn around in this narrow road, partway up the mountain and no rail at the side.

At the lower side of Hunter's Mountain was one of the worst turns in Cape Breton, known across Nova Scotia as The Devil's Elbow. Papa had warned him to use low gear. He could not imagine what he would do if he met another vehicle. He had to steer and feed out gas with one hand, while the other hand pressed his knee down to keep the car in low gear.

He was damned proud and soaked with sweat when he arrived at Nyanza. He was a successful chauffeur, driving a Rolls Royce Silver Ghost.

Alex Jim was in a great hurry.

"Where you been, boy?" he said, pulling open Archie Neil's door and sending him to the passenger side. "I can't dilly with a slow poke." He jumped in and made the return trip in record time, sweeping The Devil's Elbow with gravel flying.

Hughie Angus Lord MacDonald was the road foreman, and in his hands resided the power to distribute hundreds of dollars worth of highway jobs. His visit was only slightly less important than a visit from the Bishop. And the Bishop could not have gotten better than Momma's biscuits and tea. He spoke to Archie Neil and Papa about the weather, about the health of his family, the health of their family, recent funerals and fishing and just about anything other than the reason he came—and no one drank the tea except Hughie Angus Lord.

Finally, he announced: "Bit of gravelling going on, Archie. About four weeks of it." Hughie accepted a third cup of tea from Momma. "Thanks, Belle. Work for your horse and cart, if you want it."

"A little extra money'd come in handy," Papa admitted.

"Thought so. A good job for a good Liberal."

He bit into a tea biscuit.

"There's a job for Archie Neil, too," he said.

Archie Neil was astonished. His upper body could certainly handle heavy shovel work, but not his legs. But the money! He had never earned a cent other than by fiddling. But he had never cast a vote, and he wondered how Hughie figured he was a Liberal.

Hughie shifted in his chair, relishing his own generosity and wanting to make it last.

Hughie Angus Lord told them that the men loading and hauling gravel in truck wagons were paid a different rate than those using box carts. There were about a dozen teams hauling gravel from the pit to the road. At the road, men with shovels spread the gravel, and then horse-drawn graders did the rest. What Hughie Lord needed was a checker. The checker stayed in the pit with a list of those with teams, and as each one left with their load, he would mark them with an X. The owner of the gravel pit was given so many cents per yard of gravel and the truck wagon held a certain amount, and the box cart held about half. This way the owner of the gravel pit knew how much had been hauled away, what the government owed him.

Archie Neil could certainly do that.

It was his first job. He saved most of the money. He did buy new clothes. A little rum. Cigarettes. Kate turned out to be as avid a smoker as himself. She could not smoke in her uncle's house, or in public, so they had smokes together outside of dances, or times by the river. He thought of proposing to Kate. But how would he support her? Handling the check-off during roadwork?

At Sunday dinner, Momma was agitated about the sermon, which described the torments in Hell of Martin Luther. She had a kind heart and she was worried about poor Martin Luther, beyond the reach of prayers, for eternity. "I didn't know he was in Hell," she kept saying. "Purgatory maybe. I thought maybe Purgatory. He wrote such nice hymns for the Protestants. Archie, what did he do?"

Papa said, carefully, "He questioned the Pope, dear."

Momma looked shocked. "Dhia! Well, Father Baldwin knows who is in Hell better than I do."

Papa, Willena and Angus finished and left the kitchen as quickly as they could. Momma was upset, and this could lead to saying the rosary. But Archie Neil was in the mood for a dangerous conversation.

"Maybe Father Baldwin doesn't know."

"Of course he does. Have some respect."

"I don't respect Father Baldwin," he persisted. "Maybe Martin Luther should be a saint. This whole thing about Hell— I don't believe in it. I can see Purgatory and all that. But not Hell. Nobody is that bad. How long can a man sin? Maybe most of his life, if he tries real hard, does a little everyday. But this eternal stuff? No."

Momma sat down slowly, dismayed. Archie Neil knew he'd gone too far, but his apostasy was out of the bag. Anyway, he felt this was long overdue. He was getting old enough.

"Where did you get such ideas? What is happening to you?"

"They are my own ideas."

"And you know more than clergymen?"

"Some of them, yes. I don't think God created Hell. Priests did. And not eating meat on Friday, women wearing hats, men

t wearing hats—all of it—I don't think God gives a—" He
pped. "I don't think God cares about that sort of stuff."

"Nach tu tha bragoil," Momma said. "You're very cheeky. I
uppose you don't believe in saints, or the miracle at Lourdes?
suppose you don't believe in the Pope anymore than you believe in the word of Father Baldwin?"

"I didn't say all that."

"Well, I'll not have you questioning clergy. Not ever again."
She was really angry. "Who do you think you are, doing that?"

"You didn't like Father Fraser," he reminded.

Momma started to say that that's not the point.

"When he told the people in the church to vote against Uncle Angus. When he ripped into the Liberals."

Momma could still see her own relative pursuing the priest
to the glebe house door. Uncle Angus yelled at the priest and
everyone heard him. He told him, "You haven't got Jesus
Christ by the throat! I have three ambassadors in Heaven praying for me"—he meant his children who had died in infancy—
"and that is more than you'll ever have!"

Momma was on her feet. Her face was troubled. Her two
absolutes, the comforts of her life—her family pride and her
Catholic faith—colliding. Archie Neil thought he'd feel satisfied, but he felt ashamed.

Kate came out of John Sod's store just as Archie Neil was going in. She brushed past him without a word.

"Kate!" he called out. She had to stop.

"What do you want?"

"Maybe we could go for a drive Thursday."

"I don't think so," she said. She walked away rapidly.

He felt suddenly cold, nervous.

That evening he rode over to Kate's on Ida. Kate's cousin,
Una, answered the door. For all her politeness, she too looked
at him in an unfriendly way. "Kate is at a dance in Inverness,"
she said. "She's staying with a friend."

But Archie Neil was sure he'd seen Kate briefly at a window.

He did his work at the gravel pit lying on his belly above the
pit, marking each load. He was no longer thinking of the new

clothes he would buy when he got paid. He didn't rehearse in his head witty stories for Kate, or plot how to put her in romantic moods. He examined his conscience. What had he done wrong? Why did she and several other young people of the Forks suddenly avoid him? He could not figure it out. Confidence in himself had slipped away. Maybe she led him on, to ridicule him because he was a cripple.

He played at a dance at Belle Côte and she was there and did not once acknowledge him. So he made a show of being a merry fiddler, telling jokes to anyone who came near the stage, and putting such incredible lift into the fiddle tunes that even Angus said that he had never played better. But on the way home, in the darkness, he cried and he felt an unbearable, heavy weight in his chest. At home, he slept more, ate little, and was silent, withdrawn.

On Thursday, Archie Neil drove to Kate's in Alex Jim's car. "I'm not leaving until I see Kate," he told Una at the screen door. "I know she's here."

Una disappeared into the house, and he waited a long time. Finally Kate came to the door. She looked at him through the screen, but said nothing.

"Kate, come for a drive," he said. "I swear, if you don't want me to, I'll never bother you again. But I have to know."

"Oh, don't play such a hurt innocent," she said coldly. "You know very well. It's just, I thought I was smarter than that." Kate moved back and away.

Janet Morris, the girl who had cheated on the Provincials, suddenly came to the screen. She smiled her most disagreeable smile.

"'S math an airidh," she said, sweetly. "It serves you right."

Probably he would never find out what lies she had told.

The next summer Kate did not return to Margaree Forks. He never saw her again.

CHAPTER 15

In 1928, Archie Neil went to St. Francis Xavier in Antigonish. It was a fast, mindless year. It tested his maturity, his ability to concentrate—and he failed.

The crowd that gathered around Archie Neil all wanted the same thing. Girls, if they could find them. But they'd settle for game after game of bridge, sports—and good grades if it didn't take too much time away from their other pursuits. Archie Neil found himself in demand for entertainment and he was eager to oblige. He enjoyed the luxury of throwing his books on a table after classes and forgetting about them. It was not at all like at home, where Momma monitored his homework. He had forgotten his love of books in his pursuit of being the centre of attention.

Here, who knew or cared if he studied at all? As long as he got by. In brief moments of insight, he recognized that he was failing himself, but he dismissed it. He just didn't want to study. He forgot his ambition to be a teacher. And when he remembered, he thought about the pitiful payment Papa had received, when he actually got it in cash. A life of being paid with a side of beef, enough money for your taxes and loads of split wood could hardly compare with the wealth some people were born into, or came by in ways easier than teaching.

Archie Neil would have liked to have had good grades, just as he would have liked to have been a great fiddler—but he really did not want to work. He congratulated himself that he generally passed quizzes and tests, albeit by a narrow margin. It was easy and pleasant, he discovered, to loaf his college time away.

Moreover, he had plenty of encouragement. Bob White and Peter MacNeil would catch him after Sunday Mass, suggesting a few fiddle tunes. "I'll bring the rosin for your bow," Pete said, opening his jacket enough to show a pint of whiskey.

The plain truth was that Archie Neil lapped up their attention, flattered by what he took to be prosperous city boys who were willing to educate this country bumpkin. It didn't matter that they had nothing but scorn for all New Brunswickers and most Cape Bretoners—no use for Newfoundlanders at all. He told himself that he had the music, bait for the fish. And Archie Neil was flattered to have visitors fill his dorm room, at any hour they chose.

Travelling out was a hassle for him. The steps at the college were murder. He timed himself when he first got to the campus so that he'd know how early he'd have to start out to get to classes on time. He sweated his way up flights of stairs, using two crutches under one arm, pulling himself along by the bannister—and this in full view of students who virtually leapt down the stairs, ran up them two and three at a time.

Carrying books was out of the question. A roommate, Finlay Cameron, often arranged for someone to get the books where Archie Neil was heading. Still, it wasn't worth it to Archie Neil, to be seen like that, hauling himself up stairs. Eventually, he blamed the stairs for his poor attendance, and consequently for his low grades.

Archie Neil had times when he knew he was not only failing himself, but Momma and Papa as well. He could see Father Moses Coady sitting in their kitchen, elbows on the table and the tips of his big fingers held just together, encouraging Papa and Momma to find a way to send a boy as bright as Archie Neil to the college in Antigonish.

"You can space out the payments."

"You see," Papa told the priest, "I don't make that much in a year."

Father Coady suggested that perhaps others in the family could help. Archie Neil could see the struggle in Papa, between pride and practicality. He knew how much Momma wanted it.

How else was Archie Neil going to live in the world if he didn't make his way with his head?

Papa said, "We'll manage it somehow."

In September Archie Neil felt quite important riding with Father Coady in his shiny new black Ford, the priest's contribution to his educational costs, saving him train fare. It was not long before the Ford looked like every other car they met, grey with the dry dust of the gravel roads. They had to keep the windows closed. For Archie Neil, once past Inverness town they were entering uncharted country, passing the new-mowed fields in Mabou, Port Hood, Judique, and Creignish. From the Creignish Hills, he first saw the broad view of St. George's Bay and, beyond, the Nova Scotia mainland. Father Coady talked all the way about what this or that place had been and what it could become. From the way he was talking, it seemed that the whole future depended upon Archie Neil.

Crossing on the ferry *Edith C. Walker* to mainland Nova Scotia, he looked back across the Strait of Canso to see autumn beginning to overtake a Cape Breton Island without him. He was dressed in the suit Momma took three days to make over.

He arrived at St. FX with one suitcase, practically his entire wardrobe, a clutch of money to give the bursar and the bookstore, and his fiddle. Uncommonly quiet, he was grateful for the solid presence of Father Coady.

Moses Coady left him with the advice that he probably ought not to room with another Cape Bretoner. "Mix in with other people," he said, "but watch out what crowd you're with. Rough fellows around."

Archie Neil felt pretty sure he could take care of himself. He was a college man now. Sophisticated.

Archie Neil figured he could handle the rough fellows. Music soothes the savage—and gets them to bring the whiskey.

At first he felt left out of everything. The seniors hazed the freshmen mercilessly. All the students were in the gymnasium and it was explained to the freshmen in a humorous but insulting way that for a week they were at the beck and call of seniors, to do whatever they asked, no matter what, and if they did not obey there were unspecified penalties. And they told Archie Neil that they were leaving him alone because he was crippled.

After the meeting, Archie Neil walked to the science building with Garfield MacDonald, from Crossroads, Country Harbour. Just as they were beginning to go up the steps, four senior boys came up behind them. They ignored Archie Neil but they immediately set down some tasks for Garfield. They tied a dollar watch around his neck with a piece of old rope. He was to stand in front of the science building when the girls from Mount St. Bernard entered the building. The girls always came in a group, guarded by one or two nuns. Garfield was to jump up and down in front of them and yell at the top of his lungs: "Chase me ladies, I'm full of cornflakes."

Garfield said, "Go to hell," and they grabbed him immediately, and dragged him away. Archie Neil found out that they put him under a cold shower at the gym, fully clothed. It ruined his coat.

And, listening, Archie Neil found himself jealous.

Archie Neil invited another Cape Bretoner to his room, a Donald who happened to actually come from Bras d'Or. Archie Neil played "Donald from Bras d'Or" on the fiddle, and together they belted out the song about throwing away homespun and crooked brogans, and donning a pair of gaiters to woo the Yankee women. "Big Donald from Bras d'Or; Big Donald from Bras d'Or; Wild and crazy, drunk and lazy, was Donald from Bras d'Or." Students nearby had to come see what fun was afoot, and soon four or five were joining in the chorus. Poor Finlay, who was actually trying to study, looked upon all of this a little sourly, but put up for it this once.

He soon found the parties were going to go on and on.

"I know a way to get free smokes," Donald said. And because he was not a smoker himself, he explained how it was done. Archie Neil bought a flat of fifty cigarettes, and went through Pig Alley, the freshman dorm, selling tickets, each with a number from one to fifty. If the student drew number seven, that student paid him seven cents. If the number forty was drawn, the student paid him forty cents. When he had sold all the numbers, he then put all fifty tickets into a hat and drew one. The winner was given the flat. This generated enough money to buy two more flats, one for himself, and one for another lottery. And Archie Neil was never again without cigarettes.

There were other ways that he was learning about being poor. He met a number of students who had been to Europe, who knew because they had seen, that the Louvre was between the river Seine and Rue de Rivoli. History Professor Edward Codrington Lytle, privately known as Little Eddie Cod, viewed Paris as the heart of the civilized world, and he talked endlessly about his visit with the artist Edgar Degas who did not stoop to receive many visitors and whose sarcasm he deemed proof of his genius. "The notion," Lytle was fond of saying, "of country bumpkins pulling themselves up by the bootstrap of education, is valid only if you teach them the trades, how to use their hands. Trying to educate their minds is like educating the natives of Borrio-boola-Gha." He would say this and he would laugh. He sometimes parodied student papers, pointing out the "bumpkinisms." And while Archie Neil would have enjoyed bumping Little Eddie Cod, he sometimes could not help but think that Professor Lytle had him pegged.

Archie Neil knew that he could do the work. He had a good, retentive memory. He went to most classes. But he hated to spend these endless hours alone with the damn books.

Despite the lack of money, and the pesky business of classes, Archie Neil was beginning to have a pretty good time.

His roommate Finlay Cameron was from Mabou, a first string football player. The regulars in his room included tall, rangy Bob White from Shediac, New Brunswick, who was a good hockey and football player; Peter MacNeil, a Glace Bay boy, another hockey player, smaller than the others but physically tough; Dempsey Chisholm, the runner and hammer thrower; and live-wire "Stelly" MacIsaac. H. P. MacKinnon was there, and Tony O'Neill. Steve MacGillivray played with him at times even though he was classically trained.

J. Clyde Nunn was an occasional visitor. He loved the Irish tunes that Archie Neil played. Nunn planned one day to be a radio performer, had already worked in the field.

Many of his visitors were upperclassmen who, like Edgar Degas, did not often stoop to visit inferiors, and most emphatically not freshmen. But they visited Archie Neil.

Archie Neil sat on one of the chairs in his room while the other boys sat on the floor or sprawled across his bed. It was just the kind of setting Archie Neil loved. He was the centre of attention. And as far as he was concerned, he had the rest of the day for music and a few drinks with friends. He put books right out of his mind.

"Make yourself to home," Archie Neil invited, quite pointlessly. "There are no bedbugs there."

Bob looked at him strangely. "I hope not."

"There's boarding houses in Cape Breton where you might find one or two," he went on. "But not here, not here."

Pete took a long swig, and with the lazy, careless voice of one anticipating a pleasant Sunday afternoon of idleness, commented, "Out with it, old man. I can smell one of your lousy stories."

Archie Neil had a turn at the bottle. "Well, this fellow named Big Donald was working in the woods away from home and he was looking to stay in this boarding house. The one thing he hated more than anything else was bedbugs. So he asked the woman who ran the house if there were any. She said no. This didn't satisfy him, so when he saw the hired girl in the hall, he asked her, 'Are there any bedbugs in this place? You change the beds, you ought to know.' She said no. He was still suspicious. So he asked one of the other woodsmen who had taken a room there the day before. 'Only one,' he said. 'Only one?' 'Only one.' 'So,' the fellow said to him, 'I take it you had a good sleep?' 'My God no,' he said. 'I was awake all night because of the wake.' 'Whose wake?' 'The bedbug's wake. He died, and hundreds of his relatives came to pay their respects.'"

Bob threw the pillow at Archie Neil. "Gawd, I hate Cape Bretoners."

He passed the pint back to Archie Neil. Just then, there was a knock at the door. Everyone jumped, and Archie Neil, in a panic, slipped the bottle behind him on the chair. Bob pulled opened a window to let out the fumes, and Pete, after lighting a cigarette, opened the door.

It was Father Morris Tompkins from North East Margaree with Bishop MacDonald. The Bishop was visiting the university, conducting Sunday services. Cigarettes were hastily butted out.

Introductions all around, with formal courtesy. Polite questionings. Transformations into earnest young men. Academic matters. Career aspirations. Archie Neil sitting very straight, nodding toward his crutches across the room as his excuse for not getting up, inviting the newcomers to sit in the two remaining chairs. He knew that everyone wanted to know the reason for this visit.

"The Bishop would greatly enjoy a few of your Cape Breton tunes," Father Morris said. "I thought you wouldn't mind, Archie Neil."

"Not at all," Archie Neil said too quickly. "I'd be delighted. It would be an honour." He started to get up to get his fiddle from the desk, and then sat down heavily, remembering the bottle.

"I'll get it for you," Bob said. "I'll get it."

"Any requests, Father?"

"Oh yes, 'The Irish Washerwoman,'" the Bishop said, with a smile, "I love that tune. And 'Lord MacDonald.' Do you play that one?"

"Two favourites," Archie Neil said. He played requests for over half an hour, while Bob and Pete sat like soldiers on the edge of the bed.

As the two priests left, the Bishop complimented Archie Neil's playing. "I noticed too," he said, "that you sit so very nice and straight for a left-handed fiddler. Keep it up, Archie Neil!"

Archie Neil did keep it up. He played fiddle all weekend, and at least twice during the week.

One night, Bob, Pete, Clyde Nunn and a newcomer, Alan Power from Antigonish town, were in his room, and Archie Neil's roommate Finlay, in a rare display of temper, said, "This is getting to be a bloody daily ceilidh," and left slamming the door. Archie Neil resolved to cut down. But it was difficult. People wanted him, and he was having a good time.

This night, Alan Power listened to him play two or three tunes without much enthusiasm. "I know quite a bit about Scottish music," he said, "and I don't know what that stuff is you're playing. Your cuts are bad. Your double cuts are worse. Maybe it's all right for a bunch of Cape Breton drunks on the dance floor, but I wouldn't cross the street to hear what you play."

"Shut up," Bob White said, realizing this fellow was serious. It was one thing for him to rake over his Cape Breton friends. It was another thing for the newcomer to shoot off his mouth.

Archie Neil didn't say a word. He had never actually heard criticism of his playing before.

"No, I won't," Alan persisted. "Look how stiff his fingers and wrists are. His playing is a joke."

Bob was on his feet.

"Never mind," Archie Neil said. "Criticism is the soul of envy."

"Well, Alan can just go," Clyde Nunn suggested. His tone was casual, calm. "Sorry you don't like it, Alan, but we sure enjoy Archie Neil's music."

"I wouldn't call it music at all," Alan persisted.

Maybe it was the liquor. Maybe it was the snot-nosed mainlander who just wouldn't let up. But in any case Bob hauled off and struck Power a clumsy blow across the face, sending him down sprawling against the door. Power didn't get up right away, but he called Bob a jerk. Said they were all a bunch of jerks. And Archie Neil wished he had his crutch in his hands. It was a great weapon. But he walked with a cane now. It was one of his few lasting achievements during his year at college. Joe Basha from Newfoundland convinced him to try his cane, once Joe's broken ankle healed. Archie Neil practised in the gym. With the cane in his right hand, the broken hinge of his left knee threatened to land him on the floor. But the cane in his left hand stabilized him, and eventually he could walk as well as with crutches. Joe gave him the cane, and the crutches ended up under the bed. But unlike crutches, a cane wouldn't be much use against Alan Power.

As it happened, Power was in no hurry getting up. He still felt he was right about Archie Neil's playing and about crazy

Cape Bretoners, but he wasn't going to take on a roomful. He worked himself up, standing right against the door.

"I heard your brother Angus play," he said softly. "A much better fiddler than you"—and he shot out the door.

In February, Papa sent him a letter. He was sorry but he was unable to send any more money. Archie Neil would have to come home before the end of the term because he could not make the third payment.

"If your parents don't come up with at least part of the money, I'm afraid you'll have to leave." Archie Neil left the administrator's office feeling humiliated and resentful. He felt that his parents had let him down.

To make it worse, Dr. Coady came to his room with a lecture, disappointed that he was not using his potential. Archie Neil told him that he did hope to somehow finish the year, but Dr. Coady left without any concrete advice as to how the third payment might be made. Archie Neil wanted to be angry but he knew what Dr. Coady said was nothing but the truth.

He made another appointment with Mr. Holland. Cold and nervous, he avoided the eyes of large framed photographs of priests that lined the office wall, while he stood there and told Mr. Holland, "I'm going to be a teacher. I need a loan. I will pay it back, every cent, when I am teaching. You have my word."

Mr. Holland could give him no guarantees.

Archie Neil went on with his classes with bleak determination. He turned his back on the temptations of fiddle and fellowship, and studied most days until the library closed. He expected any day to get notice that he was dropped from class rolls. Nothing came. He finished out the year.

When he got his final grades, he had failed Latin and science. He also got notice of the tuition money he still owed.

PART TWO

CHAPTER 16

This is Archie Neil speaking:

In the summer of 1926, after I came home from college, I got a good welcome, which I enjoyed—the student coming back from St. FX. But I felt that I had let my parents down by failing two subjects. My father and mother were disappointed, as well as Dr. Moses Coady, who had helped me get into college. It was hard for my parents to afford sending me to St. FX: a large family, bills to be paid, not much money.

I was asked to play at quite a few weddings and dances. Angus was playing more than I was, because he was a better player. But I got along with everybody and was popular because I was ready for any type of fun. Even questionable fun. I wanted to be with the boys at any cost, even though I felt myself to be not quite as good as they were.

In the summer of '26, almost every chance I got to have a drink, I'd have it. I don't think my mother and father had caught on to this yet, though they did catch on where Angus was concerned. I was able to bluff them only so long. We weren't the only ones—practically everyone in our age bracket at that time would take a drink whenever possible.

I wanted to get away from home and get earning my own money. I had Grade 11, and one year in university.

About August 15, I picked up *The Casket* one day and I was reading Want Ads when I saw an ad "Teacher Wanted" for Argyle School, applicants please phone A.B. MacDonald, who I believe was school inspector at the time. Later he became prominent in agriculture and with the co-operative movement.

The next thing was, where could I phone from? I didn't want anybody knowing, especially my parents. I thought the quickest way was to write him a letter, and I did, outlining my qualifications. I got a letter back right away telling me I had the job. I was to take the train to Antigonish, and from there go with the mail driver, who had a "truck" (actually, it was a passenger car). Then I would get off the truck at South River Lake at John A. MacNeil's, who was the postmaster. MacNeil was also a trustee of the South River School. Argyle was a border section, part of it was in the District of St. Mary's, part of it was in Guysborough, and part of it was in Antigonish. You had to make three returns, but I didn't know that at the time.

I had fairly good clothes, I had a fiddle, but I didn't have one cent of money to go away. My father and mother did not want me to go, because they thought I was too young and immature to be on my own. I went to a lady who was running a restaurant at Margaree Forks, a sister to Dr. M. M. Coady. Where Reggie's Irving Station is now, that was where she had a rooming house and restaurant. She was an excellent housekeeper and cook, and it was a popular place. We were good friends. She was a lady in her 60's then. I told her my circumstances, and asked to borrow $20.00. She asked if I would pay it back, and then without hesitation, she gave me the money.

When the time came for me to leave, I got a chance to go to Inverness to stay at my cousin's, Mattie Ferguson's.

Somebody took me down to the station at seven in the morning. I paid $3.50 or $3.75 for my ticket and I got on the Judique Flyer, and I left. This was my second time on the train.

These were the days when the train had to be taken across the Strait of Canso on the train ferry called the *Scotia*. They took the train apart in Cape Breton. The engine stayed on this side. You went across in the passenger car and they took another half hour or more to put the pieces of the train together in Mulgrave, hitch you up to another engine, and you were away.

I was excited and worried. I didn't know how far away from the school I would be living, or what I was going to teach. I didn't know what I was going to find. I was gambling on the unknown, but being a little bit brash and bold, I thought I could handle anything that came along.

I got off the train at Antigonish. I asked the first person I met where the mail truck was, the one from Antigonish to Isaac's Harbour. Ed Rood from down Isaac's Harbour was the driver. I paid him $2.50. After that I had $14.00 left. We landed in this rural area, and there were no houses visible except the post office. When I got off at the post office and announced that I was Archie Neil Chisholm, the new teacher, Johnnie MacNeil looked at his wife. His children were there. One was Jenny, about sixteen or seventeen, and the other was Donald. Jenny and Donald were to be two of my students. I couldn't understand the look that passed between Johnnie and his wife.

Johnnie said, "I'm afraid that I have bad news for you. You are one mile from the school. You have to go down this hill and turn to your left and go up a dirt road for about a mile."

He asked me then, "Can you teach Grade 11?" I said, "Yes." "Well, then, my daughter Jenny and Jean Nichols from Goshen way will be in your class," Johnnie said. Then he took his wife in the other room and I could hear them talking in undertones.

I didn't know what I was going to do. I knew that I couldn't walk the mile if there was a lot of snow. This was the first year I was really using the cane.

Johnnie and his wife came out and I will never forget the joy that was in my heart when Johnnie said, "Archie Neil, I think we have your problem solved. I drive the mail three times a week from South River Lake to Giant's Lake, and I have two horses and wagons. I will fix up the old wagon and another harness, and you will take Jenny and Donald to school—you can drive a horse?"

I said, "Yes, I spent near all my life on horseback or driving horses."

"That's all I want to know," he said.

He said if I would teach Grade 11, he would see that I had transportation to school. On Monday morning Donnie, the young fellow, got the horse and wagon, and we took off for school. My first day earning my own living.

The school was small, old and leaky. No porch to it, you came directly into the classroom. The seats were all homemade double seats. The blackboard was black paint on a fairly smooth wall. The full equipment was a big stove and a box of chalk. I had a homemade desk. When I sat down at that desk, I felt ecstatic. I couldn't be happier. My transportation problem had been solved and I was good for the year.

I had from Primary to Grade 11, about nineteen students. I wanted to make this year a success!

CHAPTER 17

The English language was Hector Dan MacGillivray's enemy. He was twelve years old and he figured that the subject had it in for him. Way back, some dumb old people started doing stupid things to English, just to make his life miserable. Teachers tried to drum the grammar into his head. But he always wanted to know the why about things. All they usually told him was "It's in the book," just like church, even when it didn't make any sense to him at all. They tried to beat grammar into him with a ruler, blackmail, nasty reports to his parents, and depriving him of recess and lunch. None of it worked.

Now this new teacher with the crooked legs was at it again.

The only thing Hector Dan really liked about school was talking to the other boys about boxing. Ever since his father bought a radio through T. Eaton's catalogue, this was his obsession. Every boxing night, a crowd of people came to the MacGillivray house to listen. Other than Hector and his father, no one dared make so much as a cough during a broadcast or they might get tossed out. Father and son gloried in it. And Hector was the authority on boxing at the school.

But this wasn't even regular school, with the other boys to talk to. A perfectly good Saturday was ruined. Hector Dan's father sent him over to John A.'s. Just for stupid irregular verbs, irregular plurals and that other garbage, he thought. Well, nobody was going to cram it down his throat.

"Thank you a good deal indeed," Hector Dan's father said

to Archie Neil, ready to leave his son behind. A burly farmer, he stood with his hat in his hand at the kitchen door. He respected teachers. They were right up there with God. "The Sullivans, they told me you've been helping kids extra, evenings and weekends. Hector Dan, he doesn't do good, grade-wise."

"We'll do fine," Archie Neil said, with a wink at the boy, one of his most difficult students. He was bright enough, and he wasn't unruly. He just wouldn't do anything he didn't want to do. And he didn't want to do anything with English grammar.

After Hector Dan's father left, Archie Neil leaned back in his chair and stretched a good, long, lazy stretch. "Listen, if you don't tell on me," he said, "we'll just—well, you know, shoot the breeze. Have a few laughs. Nobody will know but you and me. How about a cup of coffee? You take cream and sugar?"

"Yep," Hector said. "Ah—thanks." He had never been offered a cup of coffee before by a teacher. This was uncharted territory.

While the kettle came to a boil, Archie Neil said, "It was soft living that did Dempsey in. Being a movie star and all that. It was his own fault he lost."

Hector lit up. This was Dempsey and Tunney fighting in Philadelphia last September. Now this was something worth talking about.

"Naw. There's plenty of sock to Dempsey yet," Hector said. "How else do you think he lasted ten rounds?"

Hector Dan and Archie Neil sparred for awhile over which was the better fighter. Hector was getting a little respect for this teacher. His guard started down. Archie Neil jabbed:

"You know, Hector, I don't blame you one bit for digging in your heels—about grammar, I mean."

Then, more slowly, Archie Neil said, "Grammar—it's about as crazy as bedbugs in a bottle. When I'm teaching it, I can hardly stop from laughing right out. It's like it's a big joke."

He let his words seem unimportant, deliberately indistinct, chewing away at a biscuit slathered with butter. Still, Hector hastily pulled up his anti-grammar guard. He wasn't talking.

"Now don't tell the other students I told you this," leaning closer and lowering his voice. "Take for instance, mouse. More than one mouse is mice. Right?"

No response.

"Well, it is right. More than one mouse is mice, isn't it?" He got back a tentative, "Right."

"But whoever made that up was really dumb. Because then two houses ought to be hice. The same with goose. Should be gice. But more than one goose is geese. Right? Everybody knows that."

Archie Neil leaned back with satisfaction, brushing crumbs from his shirt. Where was this teacher going? He leaned in close to Hector Dan again, glanced behind him, made sure they were alone.

"But then, the idiot that made up that rule, forgot about moose. If goose is geese then moose—did you ever hear of people hunting meese?"

Yep, meese was dumb. Almost funny. Hector Dan set his mouth firmly against the smile. He didn't want to be suckered in. What was this crooked-legged fellow up to?

"Yeah," Archie Neil said, almost outraged. "If we're supposed to say, 'I do, I did, I have done,' then cows should go, 'Moo, mid, and—'"

"Have muned? mooned?" said Hector Dan. "No, have mone." At this he had to laugh. He wasn't sure if he was allowed to laugh about grammar. It would be like laughing in church. He tucked his head but he couldn't keep it back and ended up laughing into his coffee. Archie Neil got up and brought him a dishtowel to dry his face. But he did it in a manner that suggested that laughing into your coffee was totally appropriate, under the circumstances forced upon them by grammarians.

"Somebody should collect up the really stupid grammar rules," Archie Neil went on, blotting up the splatters of coffee, "and make them change them. What do you think?"

"Yep," Hector agreed.

"Then, the masculine pronouns," Archie Neil said, noting the negative look the very term produced— "he, his, and him. Based on that we should be saying she—"

"Shis and shim!" Hector said.

"Very good," said Archie Neil.

They both sipped from their cups, as if the case they were

making was sewed up in the bag and their opinion of it was beyond rebuttal.

Archie Neil stood up, locked his legs so he could stand without the cane, and poked aggressively at an imaginary grammarian with his fists. The troublemaker, disguised as an inverted floor mop in the corner near the door, did not even try to fight back. Archie Neil let him have it.

"All right, you devil, if we have to say, 'I lose and I lost,' then we should be saying 'I choose, I—' Go on, give it to him, Hector Dan," Archie Neil prompted.

"I choose and I chost," Hector supplied. Archie Neil whacked the grammarian on the nose.

"If the plural of man is men, then the plural of pan should be—" with an elaborate flurry of left jabs.

"Pen!" Hector finished in a loud voice.

"Case closed. The sentence is death!"

With a fatal thrust Archie Neil sent the mop clattering to the floor. He turned to his fellow boxer.

"What we need, Hector Dan, is more evidence. So people know what's going on. This stuff should be on the radio. If two foots are feet, then two boots should be beet! If teachers taught, then it should be the rule that preachers praught. It's an outrage! We'll write a letter of complaint, that's what we'll do. We'll send it to the grammar police. We'll tell them what we think of this stupid stuff."

Now Hector Dan belonged to Archie Neil. He sat down beside the boy. His tone simply said that they were in this fight together.

"Look," said Archie Neil, "it doesn't always make sense. And we're having fun here because we're breaking the rules. But you have to know the rules to know when you are breaking them. You won't soon forget that meese should be the plural for moose. And that'll help you to remember that it isn't. And next time we have coffee, we'll have just as much fun getting it right."

Word got around that the teacher played fiddle. That started as a fiasco. At his first dance, he played his best Cape Breton strathspeys and reels, but nobody was getting out on the floor.

Fred Kennedy came up to him, and asked if he could play polkas.

"What tempo?" Archie Neil whispered back.

Fred put up his hand to hide his mouth and he whistled a tune into Archie Neil's ear. Archie Neil tentatively picked it out on the fiddle, Fred still whistling, then got the gist of it. Polkas and quadrilles, it dawned on him, were what these people wanted. After that he received plenty of invitations.

Archie Neil was an occasional driver-escort for Jenny and Donnie, and the older MacNeil children. He took them to dances at Lochaber and Giant's Lake. He took this responsibility seriously, keeping a sharp eye on them and making sure they had a jolly time on the way going and coming back. It was fun. He didn't drink much at those times, just one or two.

But it seemed that at every dance someone offered him drinks. He was careful. At first he refused. He told himself that there was too much at stake; he was responsible for too much. But gradually, he accepted a few drinks, and then more. Here's one for an equalizer, he thought to himself. One Sunday night two brothers had to bring him home, one driving Archie's Neil's wagon, the other driving their own buggy. They helped him to his room, tiptoed back down the stairs and got away unseen.

Archie Neil taught that Monday with the worst hangover he could remember. Never again, he told himself, no more. But he took the drinks, anyway. Somehow the bottle got into his hand and up to his mouth at the same time he was telling himself that it was a stupid thing to do. I will have to control it, he told himself.

At a dance in St. Andrew's, Tom Chisholm and two trustees came up to the stage and asked him to consider becoming the principal of St. Andrew's School for the 1927-28 school year. It was a three-room rural school.

"I've heard excellent reports of your teaching," Tom told Archie Neil. "I don't want to be unfair to South River Lake, but we can make you an offer of $425.00 for the year."

Principal! He was not yet 21 and he was being asked to be principal of a school!

"Yes, that would be agreeable to me," he said, trying to conceal his eagerness. Then he added: "I'm going to be spending the summer at the Normal College in Truro—working on my teacher's license."

Actually, Archie Neil had been thinking about studying in Truro, but he had not made up his mind until that moment.

CHAPTER 18

In the summer of 1927, I went to summer school at the Normal College in Truro. I went for six weeks. The principal at the summer school at that time was L. A. DeWolf, himself a noted teacher. A tall, very spare man, with snow white hair and a ruddy complexion. Always had rosy cheeks. Always immaculately dressed. Always on the watch for mistakes in a teacher. When he corrected you, he did so in a nice, refined, gentle way. He was not long in this position, but he was recognized as important. He carried on seminars across Nova Scotia. The students had great respect for him.

While I was in Truro, I was on the very best of behaviour, from the point of view of drinking—just one or two drinks at a couple of parties. Angus and I were taking classes; he wanted to be a teacher too. He taught about five years after that.

We brought our fiddles to the Normal College, and they were looking for entertainment almost every night. We played together, much to the delight of all the students who found it a great place to spend an evening. This was one of the first times that the real Cape Breton square sets were danced there. About a week ago, a gentleman was in here, reminding me how quickly the square sets caught on.

After six weeks in Truro, I came home. We played for dances, and as we got more in demand, we were asking for as high as $5.00 an evening, which was considered exorbitant. But they paid it.

A great friend of mine, Alexander MacDonnell from Judique, who was a great violinist in the refined, correct style—one of the parish priests of Judique was getting a dance ready. They hired somebody else than Alex, and at the last minute, the fiddler didn't show up. Nobody wanted to risk showing up at Alexander's place because they hadn't asked him. Finally, the clergyman asked him. When he asked how much, Alex said, "Five dollars."

The priest thought that was awful. He said: "My heavens, you are not going to charge us $5.00 for playing at a dance! Look at all the men working on the highway for $2.00 a day! Working eight or nine hours!"

Alexander said mildly, "That's fine. You can go and get one of those men working on the highway to play the fiddle."

Angus and I were in the same boat. At the early picnics, there would be four or five of the very best fiddlers from all over the county. Angus and I were real amateurs then, just learning. And yet, it would devolve upon us to do the heavy work. The big fiddlers would play a square set or two, then go roaming around for a couple of hours. We were the go-fers, the storm troopers who filled in hour after hour after hour. They, the big fiddlers, were getting eight or nine dollars for the day, and we were damn lucky if they gave us two dollars apiece at the end of it. Once, we got two dollars to share between us!

The outstanding thing about my year at St. Andrew's (1927-28) was getting into a new school. I was better dressed, I had what I needed. I wanted to get a used car for two or three hundred dollars. A new Ford would be six or seven hundred. I made a down payment on a new car, but couldn't keep it after a couple of months. I had to pay my college bill, and I went to Tom Chisholm who was a trustee and secretary. The college bill was $150.00 or $175.00, and I asked him to pay St. FX like a draft, directly from my salary. After that, I realized that I couldn't meet car payments as well, and I didn't want to ask anybody to help me out.

I played regularly at St. Andrew's and sometimes at Lochaber. The people who put on the dances knew that I didn't have a car and that I was crippled and so they provided the transportation.

It was about that time, I made the happy discovery that there were occasional girls who would come out with me. They didn't seem to worry about the handicap, whether their eyesight was bad or something. At the age of eighteen, I discovered girls who did not care that I was crippled—enough of them to make my life interesting. I now was beginning to think I had a chance for a good life ahead of me.

At St. Andrew's I became gradually more and more fond of drinking. I didn't realize what an alcoholic was. It had nothing to do with my being at St. Andrew's—it was a good place. It had to do with me. I was making more money. I was only a few miles from Antigonish, and almost every night there was somebody going to town willing to pick me up.

Up to then, I never lost days or even an hour of teaching because of being hung over from drinking. In total, I probably lost less than eight days for this reason, in all my teaching career.

In 1928, I completed my year at St. Andrew's. I again attended a six-week summer school at Truro Teachers' College. At that time, it meant that you could get an extension to your license or that you could get a permissive license for one year. I was fortunate to be able to live in a boarding house within walking distance. My brother Angus was attending the session with me.

We didn't have a lot of money, but we had enough to pay our expenses and get by. In Truro, they were divided on the musical question. Some of the Cape Bretoners began to coax us to take our violin up to the recreation room, which was large, and on the first floor. When you came in the back side door, you made two turns to your right and you were in this large, all-purpose room with a beautiful floor. Most of the time, the room was used for modern ballroom dancing in the Recreation Centre. The students who were up on modern dancing formed quite a little band.

So the Capers used a basement room. The first thing we knew, there was a square set on the floor, and the next thing we knew, it was snowballing. There were more and more students in the square sets. Before the first night was over, many of those who had been upstairs in the ballroom, came down to see what the Capers were up to. There was so much noise and laughter coming from the room.

It was like Tom Sawyer and Huckleberry Finn: they came to jeer, but they stayed to whitewash. The crowd caught on to the fact that square dancing was really fun. The next night, the room was so packed, there was scarcely room to dance. Everybody wanted to get in on the act. At the suggestion of the teachers, we were asked to exchange rooms. You can imagine our pride when we were told to take the big room, and the ballroom dancers were relegated to the small room downstairs. Before two weeks were out, there were no more ballroom dancers, they were all doing square sets, and loving it. The occasional bow that we would make to modern dance was in the form of a waltz quadrille. It was very similar to square sets with the figures, but to waltz time.

Angus and I came home. I went Down North to Ingonish Beach to teach.

CHAPTER 19

M. Frazier Moreland sat with his legs crossed in the teacher's chair, his chin supported by a thumb and forefinger, every line of him suggestive of polite censure, maintaining a quiet voice and a refined manner.

He had asked to speak with Archie Neil privately at the school at Ingonish Beach.

"Thank you for coming down, Mr. Chisholm. I realize it's quite a long walk for you."

He motioned Archie Neil to take one of the student seats.

Archie Neil had received the phone call to come to a meeting at four in the afternoon. It was the Saturday before the first day of school, and he had no idea what it was about. He had already met with the trustees and the principal, with whom he felt he was on excellent terms; and he had spent the past week boarding at the Hawleys' house, preparing teaching materials.

On the long uphill walk to the school, he had a growing dread of this meeting, mostly because he could not figure why it was called.

They exchanged small talk about the weather, Ingonish Beach in winter. Archie Neil said that he didn't mind being snowbound as long as he had firewood and books.

"I just wanted you to know," Mr. Moreland finally said, "that some of the trustees are concerned. Just this morning, I received a report about you. It is being said that you—have a drinking problem. We wondered if you yourself could reassure us that the rumour is false, before the school term actually starts. We want to be fair about this."

"I am not a heavy drinker," Archie Neil said, his voice betraying shock. His confidence evaporated almost instantly. And he was angry with Mr. Moreland, his manner, the "report" from someone. His anger gave him back a little self-esteem. He wanted to know who was saying these things about him, but he left the question unasked. Instead, he said:

"My private life has nothing to do with my school work." He wasn't sure he believed that, but he said it well. The sound of confidence was back in his voice. "I have never missed a day of teaching because of drinking."

"I see."

"I consider myself a good teacher, Mr. Moreland. I take pride in that. I also depend on teaching for my livelihood. Some people like to tell stories about me that never happened."

"However, there are a number of equally capable teachers eager for this job, Mr. Chisholm. Without this problem attached."

"I have a right to know exactly what was said and who said it."

Mr. Moreland did not offer any more information. He idly pulled open the desk drawer a few inches just to see what it might contain.

"You saw my letters of reference from St. Andrew's and Country Harbour. They were more than satisfied with my work."

"Yes. Both schools say you are an excellent teacher, Mr. Chisholm. You are apparently very well liked as well, especially by the students. But it seems that even the students came to know about your weakness. It doesn't provide a good example, Mr. Chisholm, would you not agree?"

"Are you saying that I don't have a job here this term?"

"I didn't say that."

"Then I'll say it."

"Very well," Mr. Moreland said, with no change of expression. He closed the desk drawer. "Good day."

He walked out of the classroom, quietly closing the door.

Archie Neil took the *Aspy* to North Sydney, the train on to Port Hawkesbury. He didn't want to go home. He had told the people at the boarding house that he quit because the walk to the school was just too far. While they were sorry, they said that they understood. He did not know what he would tell Momma and Papa. He felt Momma would suspect it had something to do with drinking, even if she believed he wasn't actually fired. And she would be disappointed.

Momma's great power was her disappointment. She had tried badgering Angus mornings after he'd been brought home drunk, but that only led to arguments. Angus finally told her that it was his own business, not hers, and that got Papa into it, telling Angus that when he was under this roof, everything he did was family business. He came around the table and slapped Angus—and Angus just took it, tired. He looked at Papa with a flat gaze of misery. Papa knew it was useless, told him to get out of his sight—and by that time no one meant anything they said.

Archie Neil himself was fighting nausea that day, he had a headache. He knew that he was guilty, too. And he knew that Angus was not drinking to hurt Momma, or to make her ashamed. No more than he was. But he agreed with Angus. It was not Momma's business, although he would not have said that aloud. Instead, he said, "It's not your fault, Momma."

He was surprised at her quick look of gratitude, as if she had wanted him, or somebody, to say just that. Archie Neil struggled to his feet, "He'll be all right," he continued—surprised to find himself acting the tender hypocrite. He reached to take a dirty plate from her hand. "I'll finish this...."

"No," she said sharply, keeping the plate. She looked at him as if she suspected that he was trying to ingratiate himself to her, at Angus's expense. She said, "I want to be doing something."

But her look was disarming, disappointed.

In Port Hawkesbury, Archie Neil visited Aunt Christena and her husband Angus. He didn't tell anyone about the meeting with Moreland.

"It was too far to walk," he told his aunt.

"You don't look quite yourself," she responded. He told her the air on the train was bad.

But he was too quiet. No jokes, no stories. Too quiet. Aunt Christena knew that something was terribly wrong. He said that he felt exhausted. She got him settled in her son's old room. She wanted to ask about the family at the Forks, but Uncle Angus said, "Leave him alone."

The school year started without him. He passed the time as a kind of chauffeur for his aunt and uncle. He promised himself he would never take another drink.

After a few days, things seemed improved. By the third morning he was more lively at breakfast. He had decided that the least he could do, as a guest, was to allow his hosts to quit tiptoeing around him. Aunt Christena joined the men at the table, grateful that he was feeling better.

Archie Neil took a bite of toast. "I'll tell you a story: This is from the time when the animals could talk."

Aunt and Uncle listened closely. There would be a lesson here. After all, Archie Neil was a schoolteacher.

"Yes, when the animals could talk.

"There was this group of cattle were out for the summer pasture, and when they were brought into the barn in the fall, they were reminiscing about their summer. And one cow is supposed to have said to the other, 'What sort of summer did you have?'

"The cow answered, 'We had a beautiful summer. We were eight of us in a huge big pasture. The clover, the grass, was up to our knees. We had a marvellous time. And across the way,' she said, 'there was a fellow who kept bulls for sale. And the bulls broke down the fence. And that added to our joy for the summer. Personally, I never had such a good time.'

"But there was one little cow down at the end of the stable, and she wasn't saying a word. And finally they said to her, 'What was your experience?'

"She said, 'It was a terrible summer. The worst experience I ever had. Forty of us were in a six-acre field. It was scruffed off by the sheep before we got in there. We didn't see anything but ourselves all summer. Finally, one day, there was an ox jumped over the fence. And he spent the rest of the summer talking about his operation.'"

Uncle Angus enjoyed the story but Aunt Christena just smiled. Archie Neil kept talking.

"Here's another one. It's a stupid superstition, this one. If a young man signs a contract with the devil to get a job, he has to stand with a Bible on his head, from dusk until dawn—while a raven comes and plucks out the pages, one by one. If the rooster crows before the last page is gone, he gets the job, and his soul is also saved. But if the raven manages to pluck out that last page...." He finished the story that way.

Archie Neil performed for them, and for anyone who would listen. He looked toward another teaching job, getting some work playing music. But most nights, he stared at the ceiling in their son's room, wanting a drink more than he had ever wanted one. He hated himself for the wanting. But the wanting didn't stop. He recalled every stupid, humiliating thing he had ever done or said, every defect in his body and character. By the time he finally fell asleep, his thoughts were only on how his life, his whole life, felt crippled, inadequate.

God, he wanted a drink.

CHAPTER 20

Fenwick Skinner latched on to this schoolteacher fellow like a cod on a jig.

Better known as Fenny, he had met Archie Neil at Alexander Hughie T.'s when they both were boarding there, and later they came to be house guests at D. A. MacDonald's about the same time. D. A.'s wife put Archie Neil in a regular bedroom but she put Fenny in a storeroom with a cot. This was satisfactory because the storeroom was handy to the kitchen, and the schoolteacher was paying.

Since Fenny retired the *Lucy Skinner*—she was beached and overturned near the old wharf—that's the way he lived. He'd show up and announce that he was staying on for a bit. Though a few refused him, it was hard to say no; they all knew his shack at MacKay's Point had blown down in a big storm and he never saved a cent in his life. Since he stopped fishing, Fenny seemed to figure that God had made the village of Judique responsible for his keep. Let the women cook for him, he reasoned; he couldn't be bothered with that go-ahead any more. He would stay until his welcome wore too thin to warm him, then he would move on. It wasn't a bad life.

Fenny figured that this teacher fellow did much the same, boarded around, so they were kind of in the same boat.

Except the teacher had something Fenny wanted, and he planned to get it.

Archie Neil could avoid Fenny only so long. When he

looked up from his newspaper, Fenny was staring him right in the eye. Caught. It wasn't a rude stare, really one full of curiosity and interest. And now that he again had the teacher's attention, he smiled a toothless smile.

"Excuse me," he said, as if he hadn't been waiting all this time to bother the teacher. But also, "Excuse me"—meaning, I want your attention

"Not right now, Fenny," Archie Neil told him, trying to figure whether it was quicker to get up and walk away or just bury his head in the newspaper. He was sure he felt compassion for the old man. He looked at the body that even through the work-clothes and sportcoat looked caved in like his wooden boat, a shape earned from long labour in the cold and the wet. The old man often smelled bad, like old boiled ram slaughtered at the wrong time of the year.

Still, Archie Neil was certain that some other time he would show more compassion, would answer the interminable questions that needed only his nod or look to start flowing. But not now, Fenny, not today.

The old politician was coming to the MacDonalds' house— they were holding a political tea—and Archie Neil was catching up on the news, particularly on the way the election was shaping up. He had a stack of papers on the floor beside his chair.

And for two days now, every chance he would catch him alone, Fenny wanted to know the names of all the counties in Nova Scotia.

It was something good to know, he told Archie Neil. It was something you never know when you'll need it. It was something any educated person would have under his belt long ago. It was something Fenny was wanting.

And it was something, two nights ago, Archie Neil had admitted he knew.

"All of them?"

"All of them."

"God, you're smart."

All the counties of Nova Scotia, and if he wanted, he could say them off by heart. And he gave Fenny a few, just to hold him, before he managed to get away to his room.

But today, at the kitchen table, Fenny wanted more counties. He wanted them all.

"Teach me, Archie Neil." It did not sound pathetic. It was more like a soft command.

"Later, Fenny."

But Fenny kept after him. Archie Neil tried to drive him away, saying, "Didn't Mrs. MacDonald tell you to wash yourself before the tea? This is a big day, Fenny, important people coming. And you're going to need a few hours to get clean."

Archie Neil didn't like hearing himself talk that way. But he did want to read that newspaper, and he did want everything to add toward making a good impression on the old politician.

And it was true that Mrs. MacDonald was getting disgusted with Fenny, at least for today. She watched him pour tea into the saucer, drinking it with loud slurps. His fingernails were just plain dirty. She stood there gathering up her last reserve of patience into a very tight ball of yarn, tucking it in her apron for the future. The ball of yarn was getting very small indeed. Her husband knew pretty well the exact size of that ball, for he had been watching her wind it tight since he brought Fenny home "for a few days."

This morning Mrs. MacDonald was a lot like Archie Neil— she'd have time for Fenny some other day. But the idea of a gathering in her home turned her to what she considered more elegant ways. She was proud that D. A. was a prosperous businessman, and that their home had recently become a kind of unofficial headquarters for members of the Conservative Party in this part of Cape Breton. It was going to be a tight race in Inverness County. She had cleaned the house, polished her silver, the china was ready and the spare bedroom waiting, if the old politician chose to stay.

And then there was Fenny.

Archie Neil and Mrs. MacDonald were sort of allies. It was not something they talked about, probably not something of which she was aware. But Archie Neil sympathized with her mortification when Fenny mingled with important people who came to the house. Fenny would have something to say. It made sense at first. He did not read very well, but he'd pick up snatches of talk around the house. Things someone else had read in the newspaper would give him a fairly interesting first line. But once he caught someone's ear, he was likely to turn to babble. And people would walk away or look at Mrs. MacDonald as much as if to say, "It must be a trial to have your father living with you." How else explain Fenny in this charming home?

Archie Neil was embarrassed too. It wasn't his house, but he wanted everything to go well for his own reasons. He had come to believe that his future would be virtually assured, if the old politician were elected. Look at the change that had come just by sometimes serving as his chauffeur! People took special notice of Archie Neil when he came in next to the politician, sometimes even when he was alone. He'd get a hearty handshake, the bending in to listen intently, those significant looks. This wasn't just fiddling and jokes. One brilliant line of repartee could set a whole room laughing. He was rubbing elbows with people who had or would have power. And he would have a part in that.

And Archie Neil did not mind that political life often included plenty to drink, whether in the Tory or in the enemy camp. He was cautious when he knew he had to drive, but other than that, he had access to all he could hold, and without spending a dime.

He was alert for every introduction. Each one might lead to that vital connection. Archie Neil knew that being the old politician's chauffeur was only a beginning. They would see his true value.

But for now Archie Neil sat at the kitchen table trying to read a stack of newspapers, studying every nuance of political slant. He had a great memory. He could remember what politicians said last month or even last year, on just about every issue. He tried to prepare for the tea, but Fenny would not leave him alone.

"What county you from, Archie Neil?"

"This one. I'm from Margaree Forks."

Fenny took this in, turned it around. "Is that right?" He looked surprised. "That's not a county."

"That's right. This is Inverness County."

"Inverness County." Tuck that away. Inverness. Victoria. Even Cape Breton County is a county. He had that down solid.

"Now they's Frenchies there? Inverness County."

"Yeah."

"And some over to Madame Island. Frenchies too."

"Isle Madame. That's right, Fenny. And that's in Richmond County."

"Richmond County. Still in Cape Breton."

"Still in Cape Breton. We'll finish the mainland tomorrow."

"So what's just the other side of the Strait?"

"Tomorrow."

Richmond. Inverness. Victoria. Cape Breton County is a county in Cape Breton Island. But there's no Nova Scotia County. He had that straight.

Then Fenny got Digby, Guysborough, Halifax—just like that. Archie Neil was able to name them without looking away from a column written by a Conservative who insisted that the qualities that defeated MacKenzie King in 1911 would defeat him as roundly in 1930. Archie Neil filed that away. It would be something interesting to say.

Fenny mentioned that it was marvelous, how Archie Neil could teach him and read the newspaper at the same time. Archie Neil decided that Fenny couldn't read at all. Again, he assured himself that some other time he would take particular interest in that, even do something about it. But Fenny had just picked the wrong day.

"What do you see over the water, Archie Neil?"

"Antigonish."

"That's a trick, Archie Neil. I been to Antigonish."

"It's also a county, Fenny. Like Yarmouth is a town in Yarmouth County."

And so it went on until Archie Neil abruptly bundled up some newspapers and went to his room.

The big parlour of Mrs. D. A. MacDonald was splendid that late July afternoon before the election. Everything was fresh and gleaming, cut flowers caught the sunlight on their tables, the flowered carpet was spotless, the window was open to let in a pleasant breeze, and teacups and napkins, sweets and small sandwiches graced a buffet. She had wonderful taste and the money to indulge it. For the past few days, her house had been frenetically busy and she had hired help to keep up with the stream of visitors. There was an important meeting in Port Hood today, a debate between the candidates, and afterward the Conservatives were to come for a luncheon and a strategy session toward the next round. Their wives were coming as well.

Fenny had wandered off to one of the neighbours late in the morning and hadn't returned. Mrs. MacDonald was not disappointed. She told Archie Neil that he had gone off excited about the counties.

"I'm afraid I'm at fault. I taught him the names"—making a little more of the lesson.

"Anything to keep him amused," Mrs. MacDonald said, "and out of the way."

An hour later, Mrs. MacDonald returned to the kitchen to fill the silver teapot. The first guests had arrived from Port Hood. They talked quietly in the parlour, waiting. Archie Neil was among them.

A commotion started in the lane where about a dozen cars were parked—the old politician was arriving—and Mrs. MacDonald brushed out the door in a mild, delighted panic. She did not like what she saw.

They couldn't park the car. Fenny was right in front of it. He was waving a big sheet of paper that later turned out to be the map of Nova Scotia, and shouting to the passengers about "Cumberland, Colchester—"

Two men started to get between Fenny and the people getting out of the car, but he ducked down, scrambled, and popped up two cars over.

"Who is that crazy man?" someone asked on the porch, and Archie Neil told him that it was MacKenzie King's campaign manager—and that got a good laugh around him. But everyone still watched Fenny, who dodged around the cars and came up from behind the tired politician.

Fenny had him. He was reciting the counties of Nova Scotia. He was telling him where his people came from. Archie Neil knew he could never get across the porch and down the steps fast enough to save the politician. He could hear Fenny telling him that Archie Neil was his friend. That he was a teacher. That he drove chauffeur for a politician sometimes.

127

"I never talked with no teacher. No. Never went to school a day. My mother and father, they come over from Longton-on-the-Ribble—that's in Lancashire—in eighteen hundred and fifty-three. It's on the map all right enough. Not this one. Hard by the Irish Sea. These are the counties of Nova Scotia. Fished is what we all did. A fella ain't educated he don't know his counties. I owe everything to Archie Neil. Look!"

People tried to stop him but the old politician was absorbed in what Fenny had to say. He raised a hand in the air to no one in particular, to indicate he was listening and that he was not to be disturbed. And Fenny never stopped talking about the counties to this most important man.

Some people still tittered on the porch, but Archie Neil could feel the air of embarrassment and intrusion fading from just about everyone except himself and Mrs. MacDonald. D. A. had got to the politician's side and had one hand on Fenny's shoulder, and while the politician stayed fixed on Fenny, Fenny got the message that his time was up. He said something about his neighbour needing his map back. Something about—but it was lost, and he moved out of the politician's way.

Mrs. MacDonald got to D. A. and together they started the politician to the porch and toward just the chair she wanted him to have, and while he smiled at people who made comments or offered a hand as he passed, his thoughts were clearly elsewhere.

Fenny had done it. He had rhymed off all eighteen counties, pointing to the wrong place on the map every single time.

In the parlour, there was a flurry of greetings. "Archie Neil introduced us to MacKenzie King's campaign manager," someone said, and Archie Neil was gratified to hear the laughter. D. A. whispered something, explaining more about Fenny.

Mrs. MacDonald said she was sorry that had happened and the old politician said right back, "That's the best thing that has happened to me since this campaign started." There was laughter and, not paying attention, Mrs. MacDonald assured him that it would not happen again.

The old politician sat forward in his chair. He had a cup of cold tea in his hands. He was quiet a long time. And for the rest of the afternoon, he often turned the conversation back to Fenny.

"He's a man who has fished all his life, yet he lives in great poverty. Have any of us worked as hard as that man?" Later: "Now he's too old to fish, and he doesn't have the dignity of a home or independence. Why do you think that is?" And to Archie Neil, quietly: "Where are they living, the ones who do not have the kindness and charity of a D. A. and his good wife?"

And when he was asked to say a few words to end the gathering, he did not even try to rouse the crowd regarding the election. He went back to Fenny. "How many ragged men have you seen this past year on the rail cars? There is no bottom to it, you know. Wages cut, cut, cut until a man can work twelve hours a day and get nothing for it but a bowl of bad soup. It's already there. Black Thursday was just the beginning, my friends. The worst is yet to come.

"Why are so many of our teachers, like Archie Neil here, homeless itinerants with no security in their jobs? Why didn't Fenny have a chance to learn until he was a grown man? Is not Father Tompkins right when he accuses our institutions of being so rigid and remote that they are fortresses against our people?"

He talked about Fenny as a kind of explorer who just discovered the counties of Nova Scotia, and that is the most exciting thing of his life. How narrow was his world! How dark it was! And now there's a crack of light.

Mrs. MacDonald was sure she was going to be ill.

All in all, it was a terrible day for Archie Neil, any way he twisted it. He had survived it, but he went to bed heavy with the idea that swarmed over him during the politician's speech—the idea that he may not be so different from Fenny, estranged, handicapped. He spit the idea out of his mind. He would go somewhere in politics. He was, after all, a schoolteacher. Archie Neil found himself angry, lying there, and scared.

A few days later at three in the morning, Archie Neil went to bed a little drunk and very happy, knowing that R. B. Bennett had been elected and that the Conservatives were in power. An hour later, the old politician and his wife came into his dark room and woke him. They shook his hand. They thanked him for his support during the campaign.

"Archie Neil, my wife and I want to personally thank you for all the hundreds of miles you've driven on our behalf." They said they were leaving to meet the train. "I just didn't want to leave without saying thanks."

After they left, Archie Neil kept himself awake wondering what portion of the patronage pie would be reserved for him.

It turned out that the line-up to the trough was long. A month passed and nothing happened. Expecting something better, Archie Neil had neglected to search for a school, and now he had no job and no choice other than to go home to Margaree Forks.

CHAPTER 21

You might have wondered by now why Archie Neil Chisholm is a Conservative when the Chisholms come from a long line of Liberals. I would like to say it was because of some deep convictions or something like that. It wasn't. If I had grown up in a Conservative family, I might be Liberal now. I had this thing in me that was pretty stubborn and wanting to be different. I really thought I was thinking for myself. I didn't like a lot of what I saw about politics when I was young. You know, politicians who couldn't give you the time of day, suddenly coming to your father's house with a bottle, a glad-hand, and a line of bull. I didn't give my father enough credit. I thought he was being suckered in and I didn't like it. I constantly heard about patronage among the Conservatives, but as I got older, I knew it was a Liberal problem too.

In 1930, after the Bennett election, I didn't have a school to go to, so I came home. I wasn't completely broke, but close to it. I had the fiddle, and could pick up quite a few dollars by playing two or three times a week. In the winter time, it was not so good. There was enough change to buy cigarettes and so on.

The fiddle has played an extremely important part in my life. It was my dream at first to be a great player, like my

131

brother Angus, but you know, Kipling said, "If you can dream and not make dreams your master...." I was satisfied with just the dream. I had lots of wishbone, but no backbone. All I had to do to make things count for me was to give up that drink, and my closest friends told me to do it, for the sake of the talent I had. But I did not think I had any talent, and it was too exciting in the Roaring '20s and the Hungry '30s, and I was young, and I loved drink and good times. Every little thing counted day by day, but I didn't see it.

In 1930 the country was filling up with strangers, men walking with knapsacks on their backs, and in rags, who asked for something to eat. We didn't have much at home, but we had a roof and food, and we shared when we could.

I think they should have called those years the Impression. They certainly impressed everybody who went through them, and if you ask the survivors of it to this day, you will get an earful. The one who hears the stories either doesn't believe them, or rolls his eyes. Oh no, more crap about doing without and making do, about bootstrap Christmases, and picking old thread out of clothes. Oh, you won't believe it if you were born after that time. But there are a few things that stick to you like glue.

One of them was that every month the secretary for the school trustees went around to the households in the section to collect the tax that went for the teacher's salary. Papa's assessment was ten dollars, and there were times now when there was not a dollar to give. They all knew that the teacher sometimes did not get paid for months on end. Well, I already knew what it was like, and so did Papa.

I also remember the damn jar over the kitchen stove. Momma kept it there to collect change for household things we needed—maybe a spool of thread, or sugar, or maybe because she really needed new shoes. Usually, it was spent on the school taxes.

The few coins that jangled in my pocket after a dance jangled my conscience because I knew I should put them in the jar. But I was saving up to dribble my pocket change away in pints and quarts. Every time I lit a cigarette, it was the nagging guilt that the money should have been put in the jar. God, a fellow had to have some fun.

Music was part of me and my family. But it didn't take over, become an obsessive part of me until I was in my twenties—around 1932-33. I loved playing the fiddle for square sets, but I wished that I could take that fiddle and throw it a mile, and get up and dance with the rest. Then a little pride would take over, and I'd say to myself, "O.K., they can dance, but I can play." That was the panacea, or remedy, when I thought of the inadequacy of my physical condition.

There was no use in my dating until I had my own car. The first car I owned was repossessed because I couldn't keep up the payments on it, and the second car was pretty well shot before I bought it, and it didn't last long. I knew that if I gradually saved up, I could probably afford a down payment—you only had to put a hundred dollars down back then—and buy it on time.

I had strength to fight sickness and overcome some of the effects of the polio; I had the strength to get out and make my own living; but I did not have the strength to say no to liquor. Something terrible would have to happen to make me stop drinking, and I just didn't want to yet. But there were times when I buried my face in the pillow, ashamed that I did not have a cent of money, and that opportunities for me to go on trips or to enjoy myself with people my own age had to be forsaken. I was too proud to bum money or be an expense to someone else. Youth is resilient, but there were so many instances when I felt crushed.

The year and a half I spent at home was a repetition of all the years I spent at home since I was 16. Play at a dance, play at a concert—a great deal of it free work, gratis—come home, spend a day or two with a friend, come home sick and hungover. Clean up, and be ready for another dance. Nothing but a good time. It was a sort of sieve through which I strained the things that were bothering me.

I would sit and try to analyze myself: "You're broke, you're not of much account in the world. The only reason people come to you is that *they* want a good time, to get the music and entertainment. They didn't come for me. But a half loaf is better than none." I kept looking for that elusive thing called self-respect, blinding myself to the fact that this big wall of friendship I had around me was not real. But I refused to make a lesson in all this.

I was notified during that year (1931) that as of 1935, there would be no more permissive licenses granted. So I had to make my way, somehow, to save enough money to go to Teachers' College. At Country Harbour and St. Andrew's I was making $425 a year, but here at Portree I was making $300 a year. The board—you couldn't get better at the Waldorf—was $10 a month. How could I live? A good pair of shoes was $2.00, a nice suit was $15, a dress shirt for $1.25. Prices were cheaper than now.

When I finished at Portree in the spring of 1934, I still only had my Grade 11. There were no student loans, no help like there is now. Maybe if I had been able to put $50 a year away for several years, I could have gone to Teachers' College, but I was only living for the day. When I looked towards the longer range, I realized that I could not make an adequate living with just Grade 11. I stayed home in the summer of '34, enjoyed the good times, played at all the dances I could. Wherever there was a concert, or a benefit dance, I always got the call because they knew I wouldn't charge if there was a charitable cause. I was proud to be the one called.

Every Saturday night that summer, I played with my brother Angus at St. Patrick's Hall, North East Margaree.

134

Despite this carelessness about considering the future, I was hit with this great idea. Why couldn't I study Grade 12 at home? I didn't know what it would mean to my parents. It actually turned out well. I helped my mother during that year, and never once did she have to get down on her knees to scrub a floor. I did it for her. When I accumulated a few bucks, I contributed a small amount of groceries. When the butcher or the peddlar came around selling, I'd buy some according to what I had for money. But if I was down to seven or eight dollars, I kept it in reserve for liquid refreshments.

About the middle of August (1934) I looked up in the *Journal of Education* what subjects I would have to take. Algebra, geometry and trigonometry were written as separate subjects, not under the heading of "mathematics" as they are today. That was three subjects. There were two English tests that had to be taken.

The toughest book we had in English was Bradley's *Making of English*. You were given a resumé of all the important words that have come into English from Italian, German, French, Dutch, India, South Africa, Australia—all over the world. English is a bastard combination of many other languages. We had to study that along with other subjects in English. We also had an outside reader that we had to know from cover to cover. It was Scott's *Kenilworth*. I got that, the mathematics, the French books, the science books, physics and chemistry, economics—in all, I had to write eleven papers for the Provincial Examination.

I set up a timetable for myself, I think the only wise thing I ever did up to then, and regardless of how hung over I was coming from a dance, or how late I played at a dance, or what work I volunteered at home, I studied every day a set amount of time.

Angus decided to take Grade 12 also, so we did it at the same time. But he went to the Margaree Forks School, and

I studied at home. Angus decided that until he got his Grade 12, he would not take another drink. He stuck to that. I didn't. Occasionally, studying for me was a terrible task. At the end of that school year we both graduated.

I was going on to 28, and Angus 27.

CHAPTER 22

"Green wood, Mr. Chisholm." Alex clomped into the Widow Lord School with an armload of split wood from out back. He had the important job of feeding the fire. He had a lanky man's body but a child's mind, fifteen and in Grade Two. Archie Neil had given him the job of lighting the fire each morning, and sweeping. Alex could do a job once he was told, and he was proud of the responsibility. And at the end of the school year it was supposed to bring a little money.

"We'll get some heat out of it," Archie Neil said, picking a piece of mossy bark off the boy's wool cap.

Last night, one of the men of the school section delivered a load of wood. Most of the chunks were big and unsplit, and all of it was green and wet. It would be smoky, hard to light, and would clog the stovepipe with creosote. More than one small schoolhouse had burned down from a chimney fire

The school section was failing Archie Neil in other ways too. He had received no pay from September through December. He had ordered a twenty-dollar suit from Halifax, his first in years. It would arrive C.O.D. any day now, and he would have to send it back. Otherwise, his expenses were minimal. He lived with his uncle and paid nothing for board, a sort of exchange for helping his cousin with high school studies. But three months, and not even a dollar's pay!

He would be willing to play for quarter dances to raise money for his own wages—he'd done that at other schools—

but he wished the idea would come from a trustee or any of the parents.

But that wouldn't be settled this morning—poor wood and a damned cold day.

"Go look in the woods, see if you can find some small dry branches for kindling. Tear birchbark off a tree."

There were forty students in the Widow Lord School, a small building entered right from the road. There were hooks by the door but no cloakroom, and in winter the softwood floor was always wet. It was furnished with twenty double desks, a plate iron box stove, the teacher's desk, chair, and a map of Canada. The white walls were now a dunny smoke grey, one wall painted black for a board. In the one room Archie Neil taught Grades 1 through 11.

The school got its name because there were so many Angus MacDonalds in the region that one of them, said to have been rich, got the nickname Lord—Angus Lord MacDonald. His wife was Mary Angus Lord, and when he died she became simply Widow Lord. So when her grandson, the fiddler Hughie Angus Lord MacDonald gave the land for the school it became the Widow Lord School.

It was a sluggish, smoking fire that greeted the scholars. The day was so cold there was frost on the inside wall. They huddled around the stove, but there was little danger of scorching their clothes. Helen Marple's teeth chattered. She seemed too tiny to have much body heat. She pressed in next to Maggie Brady who wore a coat that was not warm enough for this weather. Maggie was pale and coughing. Eventually, everybody crowded in close.

"Tell you what," Archie Neil said. "We'll get the fire hotter. Alex, bring in extra wood to dry out. We'll just sit around the stove for awhile."

They stoked up the fire, pulled a few desks to sit on and sit in, staying close to one another and the stove, while Archie Neil read to them Robert Service's poem about one man's battle to get warm. "'There are strange things done in the midnight sun,'" he read in a rich, round, practised voice, "'By the men who moil for gold; The Arctic trails have their secret tales, That would make your blood run cold...'" He read it dramatically, as he had been inspired by the teaching of A.T. Jewett in Truro and Father R. K. MacIntyre of St. FX, who insisted that good speech was the first mark of an educated man, and that "Speech was not talk." He badgered Archie Neil for turning his Campbells into camels. Now Archie Neil used his strong, expressive voice unabashedly, like an actor, and it was very seldom when he read that he did not capture his audience. Knowing this fed his energy, until he was living it with the children, warmed in the glow of Sam McGee's cremation and the kind of gathering Archie Neil loved.

He went on to read Edna St. Vincent Millay's "The Ballad of the Harp Weaver," and with the verse "The wind, with a wolf's head, Howled at our door, And we burned up the chairs And sat upon the floor," the wind whistled in under the door. Most of the students were caught in the web of this poetry.

When he finished, Neil Ban MacDonnell wanted to read the Service poem again for himself, and Maggie Brady asked to try the Millay book. Archie Neil felt sure that she would memorize some of those moving words, and carry them as part of herself as long as she lived. As he read he could almost see Maggie etching the images in her mind, the recognition that, yes, she too had heard the wind howling in just like that. She often spent days in a kind of grey hopelessness. She always had a cough, week after week. She was unwell and that was it, there was nothing that could be done. Her parents were poor and the home was drafty.

"Bull," muttered Gussy, under his breath. His real name was Fergus. He left the gathering after the reading and went back to his cold seat, thwacking Alex with a knuckle on the back of the head as he passed. "Snotface." Alex just sat there. He was smart enough to be afraid of Gussy's meanness.

Archie Neil knew that Alex was Gussy's puppet. Anytime he wanted Alex to dance, he'd chuck one or two pennies out onto the floor. The sound of them was like crinkled paper to a cat—and Alex would bolt out of his chair and across the floor, scurrying after the pennies. He couldn't help it, and the teacher's firm words to remain in his seat were forgotten the moment pennies began to rattle across the floor. It wasn't just the mon-

ey, it was the sound. Archie Neil knew that Gussy was tossing
them. Probably the whole class knew. But Archie Neil had not
caught him. It didn't matter if the class would tell on Gussy,
which they would not—it would only get someone hurt later,
and telling wouldn't be the same as proof. So Archie Neil waited, and watched.

After the reading, the room now tolerable, each of the grades
began working out assignments given in arithmetic or spelling
or history, according to their level. Mary Jessie MacNeil, who
was the only Grade 11, was absorbed in physics problems,
studying hand-drawn diagrams of levers. She was a bright girl,
tall and attractive, and she wanted to be a teacher. She liked
math and science, but she resisted poetry. Especially "The Lady
of the Lake," which Archie Neil had told her to start reading.
She had looked at it, turned the pages, but her face clearly expressed distaste. She told him that she did not understand many
of the words, or any of the story. He wanted her to desire to
read it, not mechanically work through it like a physics problem, or just because it was assigned.

"I didn't start school until I was nine," Archie Neil told
Mary Jessie during time he gave to her for English. "So I had a
lot of time with my mother, listening to her stories." They had
the book open to "The Lady of the Lake," but he didn't refer to
it at all. The rest of the students were doing other work, but
some of them were listening. "I liked the stories," he continued,
"the old ones. They took me out of my bedroom and over to
Scotland. Are there stories like that in your family?"

Mary Jessie nodded. "My grandmother talks about back
there. I don't think a lot of it is true." She was serious, but she
laughed.

"What kinds of stories do they tell?"

She didn't see the point of this conversation, but he was the
teacher so she answered him. When she spoke, he decided that
she looked beautiful and probably a lot like Ellen of Douglas, the
heroine of "The Lady of the Lake" and of many of his childhood
fantasies. He quickly squelched this dangerous thought.

"Oh, my grandmother makes up what people said. How
could she remember exactly who said what? This lord, near

Portree, wanted sheep on his land. He brought a sheriff and police to kick people out, my grandmother's mother, Seana. In the winter, I think. Grandmother was her first baby, so what could she know? Anyhow, she says their neighbour's house was burning. She could see the smoke over the hill from the doorway, so Grandmother says—but I think someone must have told her. Then they were pulled out of the house. She didn't want to go. Her husband—I think his name was David or something—anyway, he was away somewhere. They threw out the bedding and furniture and stuff. She tried to go back in but the men dragged her out. She even says what the lord was wearing, and how he took the baby's cradle because he liked the carvings on it."

She told it all as her duty to tell, as something far removed and not really part of her life, and as something about which, in any event, she could do nothing. It all turned out all right. Wasn't she here now?

Archie Neil gave her an assignment. She was to talk to her grandmother, listen closely, to get the full details and to write them down. When Mary Jessie let him know that she thought that was silly, he asked her to do it, for him.

A few days later, in class, he asked her to write a composition, to tell the story in her own words. He got cold results. She seemed deliberately deficient in imagination. He wanted her to be warm, involved. He wanted her to understand, to touch something deeper in what was, after all, her own story.

"Mary Jessie, what would it have been like if you were Seana?"

"I don't know. I guess I'd have died."

"But Seana didn't. You're made of the same stuff. You're Seana, and you couldn't stop what was happening to you, to your family. There must be thousands of details that Seana would know. But your grandmother spoke of the cradle. The cradle focuses that experience, or maybe magnifies it—an exact small detail remembered clearly after almost a century."

Mary Jessie was listening to him.

"Look. I asked you to tell me about the most important event of your great-grandmother's life, and you only gave me the facts. Two plus two is four. But a cradle plus Seana—" he paused. Then: "Plus you. Write again, please, and this time see, smell, feel—as if you were Seana."

It did interest her that he was so interested in this far-off story about her great-grandmother that neither of them had ever met. It was uncomfortable. What did he want from her? What did this have to do with "The Lady of the Lake"? He was always doing that, she reassured herself, getting off the subject.

So she struggled with the assignment, for his sake, despite that it was far more difficult and much less elegant and reliable than chemistry and physics. It was too difficult. She tried to picture herself as Seana, but it was too great a leap. They both knew her composition was cold.

Then one night she dreamed of it. She saw the Lord Mac-Donald's black outline in the doorway, bold against a white background. She heard the creaking door, smelled smoke, the burning of thatch. Scotland was Margaree Forks. He had come to tear her out of her warm bed, to steal her baby's cradle. The baby struggled and screamed when it was torn from its sleep— her great-grandmother's baby, her own infant sister in a crib across the room. She was upright now, still in bed, somewhere. She tried to see MacDonald's face. She reached for an anchor, the headboard, a wall. Where was her father? She called out, "David!"

Men were in the room, grabbing up the furniture, the knot of blankets from her bed. She was brutally pulled out of her house, and it was her father's house, burning in Margaree. The wooded hill overlooking the river all blinding white. She was lost in the terror. Sensations of cold, the empty sky, the great hollow of abandonment. The panic, Seana, the cawing of a crow, the approach of darkness.

She found the headboard. She could hear her baby sister breathing across the room. She was wet with sweat, and she lay down again, listening to her bounding heart.

When she wrote the next day, she knew about Seana.

The pennies appeared sporadically, tinkling across the floor. Gussy was clever, choosing moments when Archie Neil's attention was elsewhere, or his back was turned. Alex knew very well that his teacher wanted him to leave those pennies alone, but he'd hear that sound and dart from his seat, scramble about and get them. And when he had them, it was futile to try to get them away from him. And most of the children laughed.

"Walter Scott listened to stories from his grandmother," Archie Neil told the class one day. "Like myself, he was crippled with infantile paralysis when he was a boy. They sent him to the country for health reasons, to live with his grandparents. She got him interested in the old stories, she told him about forerunners. Mary Jessie, did your grandmother ever tell you a forerunner?"

"Well, she talks about white witches and black witches, but I think it's dumb superstitions."

"Do you think anybody believes in those things?"

"I don't know."

"Now, don't misunderstand me, I'm not saying you should believe in superstitions. But there are strange things that can happen."

Maggie shyly spoke up from across the room. "I had a forerunner that my grandmother was going to die. I knew there was something there in her room when I went to say goodnight. It was black. I did, I could feel it there. And that night she died."

"My father says he had a forerunner of somebody getting married," Agnes Taylor added. "The two people hadn't even met yet, but he told them they would get married in five years. And they did."

"Okay," Archie Neil said to Mary Jessie. "Now, I would like for you to write a forerunner, make a story of one." Mary Jessie was not quick to take up her pencil, so he continued:

"Many people have forerunners. It might be part of all of us. In 'The Lady of the Lake,' Ellen Douglas has a forerunner about James Fitz-James, before she was in the boat at Loch Katrine. When she first saw him—he stepped out of the woods—she kind of backed off. But she remembered the forerunner. He was lost after his horse was killed in a hunting accident. He was the son of the King—the very King who forced Ellen's father to either hide among the steep mountains or to be killed as a traitor. And oh, a hermit prophesied about a war—the first to spill blood would be victors."

Maggie's eyes kindled with interest and questions, as did

Neil Ban's on the other side of the room. Mary Jessie glanced down at the huge, empty page, still unconvinced.

"Is it a true story?" She wanted to know.

"Well, James Fitz-James was a real person, and Ellen Douglas and her father, Lord James of Douglas. Ellen is in love with Malcolm Graeme, a nobleman who supports the king. But there was this Roderick Dhu MacAlpine—a big, strong, brave Highland chieftain who defied the King—he wanted Ellen for himself. He could be cruel and he could murder. Now, Malcolm and Roderick were fictional characters. But they weren't quite just made up either. And the struggles of the Highlanders were true, just like what your grandmother talks about. She talks about the time of The Clearances. This story is even earlier."

He let that sink in. He wanted her to know that there is truth to good fiction. He did not want her to be afraid of its magic. And he said, "You must know, Mary Jessie, that all of this leads up to us and is part of who we are today."

She looked sceptical but open. Archie Neil was satisfied with this much, for today. Let her think about it. Tomorrow, a little more....

He turned abruptly to Helen, telling her to join him at his desk. Helen had learned her alphabet and was beginning to piece together simple words. Sometimes all she needed was to sit on his lap, surveying the rest of the class. But for three days running she had baffled him. She could spell and sound out 'dog,' 'boy,' 'girl,' and other little words, but C A T eluded her. How was it different? He turned her to the black painted wall behind him that served as a blackboard. He drew a crude cat. Ears, tail, whiskers. He wrote under it in big block letters, C A T. "What is the picture?" he asked.

Helen said, "Spot." She knew she was right and smiled up at him with pride. "What does C-A-T spell?" "Spot," she said. "Cat," he said. "*Spot*," she insisted. He was stymied. A bright little thing who learned everything except the word cat.

This went on until eleven-year-old Mary Gallant gave him some help.

"Helen," she said like a mother, "tell Mr. Chisholm the name of your kitty," pointing to the drawing on the wall.

Helen said, "Spot."

"Oh, now I am embarrassed," laughed Archie Neil. "I'm so glad you were the smart one to figure that one out."

Mary drew herself up and marched away with pride.

His back was turned to the room. He heard the metallic clinking across the floor. Alex fairly leaped from his seat, crawled around under the desks picking up pennies, the students laughing at him.

"Mr. Chisholm, I found 'em. I found 'em!" Alex said coming to him, clutching about a half-dozen pennies.

The next day, there were more pennies, and this time Gussy raced from his desk to ape Alex, pretending to challenge him for the pennies. But he knew he couldn't beat Alex when Alex had the scent, and Gussy didn't seem to want the pennies anyway.

"Everyone of you, outside!" Archie Neil roared. He wanted to scream something about Alex being handicapped. He knew even Alex would not understand the indignity, and he'd only be adding to it. But he drove them out, every one of them, into the cold. No coats. Outside. "Give me a minute to cool down."

He forced his fury to subside. It only took a couple of minutes. Then he let the scholars back into the school.

Mary Gallant learned things slowly. At the beginning of the year, she came to school with matted, tangled hair; her clothes crumpled as if she had slept in them, her homework rarely finished. He couldn't seem to hold her attention. One time he asked her, "Have you been to the Indies, Mary?"

She said, "Yes, sir," but he knew she did not understaad.

He recited Burns for her. He told her that it was her poem. "Will ye go to the Indies, my Mary, And leave the auld Scotia's shore?" She smiled at that.

He decided that this one needed drastic action. So after the first month of school, he said to her, "Mary, I want you to be my Teaching Assistant."

She went home that night and told her parents that she was going to be Mr. Chisholm's Teaching Assistant, which amazed them as much as Mary. Besides her regular work, which she had to get done to keep the position, she had to draw pictures for the science and chemistry classes. He had seen her doodles and figured that she would be good at drawing. It was also her duty to help Helen Marple in Grade 1, and to work with the three Grade 2 students when they needed help at their seats. Her first job, however, was to make a cloth Teaching Assistant's badge, with TA on it. She laboured with scissors and thread for three hours. Then she washed her hair, ironed her best dress and pinned the badge on it for her first day as TA.

Yes! Now, Archie Neil knew that Mary Jessie was ready for "The Lady of the Lake." She seemed caught up in the poem, knew the intricate plot and the background. She had written of Seana with feeling, blending facts with her own thoughts, linking herself imaginatively with this mother of her grandmother so that sometimes when they spoke of it, distant tragedy was tragedy now.

"'The stag at eve had drunk his fill,'" read Archie Neil, aware of eager eyes and minds. He was himself living in it, as he had before, relishing magnificent lines, his crooked legs forgotten, his body whole and sound and riding the headmost horse all alone. "'A hundred dogs bayed deep and strong, Clattered a hundred steeds along.'" And when the labouring stag strained, "'while every gasp with sobs he drew,'" the listeners waiting breathlessly for word of his fate, glad of his escape, pitying the dying horse. Archie Neil stopped just then, to a heave of "Ohhh!" from the students. Tomorrow....

"Gussy, go out for some wood," Archie Neil ordered, the tone not at all the usual polite request. Alex was absent and the fire was low. Gussy was in no hurry, but he started for his coat. When Gussie had pulled on his coat, Archie Neil said, "Oh, wait." He tilted his chair toward Gussy. "Here, take my chair and see what's wrong with the stovepipe." There was a ninety-degree joint near the ceiling that loosened when the wind shook the chimney. Gussy got on the chair and when he raised his arms, a waterfall of pennies fell out of the cuffs of his coat-sleeves, falling around his feet on the chair, bouncing and rolling across the floor.

Nobody moved. Gussy stood there holding the pipe. And then the other children broke into hysterical laughter. His arms dropped to his sides. He didn't know what to do. He looked stupid, his face the colour of a brick.

He sparked a hateful look at the teacher, but Archie Neil was not laughing. "'Dark lightning flashed,'" Archie Neil said aloud, bringing back Mary Jessie's reading today, the fight between Fitz-James and Roderick Dhu. It was so real, the confident way she read it, "foot and point and eye opposed, In dubious strife they darkly closed." Gussy was afraid, for the first time, of this teacher who seemed the Highland chieftain who could be cruel, and who could murder.

"Gussy, you can pick up the pennies," Archie Neil said, his eyes too much like "the gleaming dagger bright" to even consider disobeying. "Pick up every one of them. There are one hundred. I want every one of them. The rest of you, get back to your work."

After school on the last day before the Christmas holidays, Archie sat at his desk, a little despondent. He was waiting for Helen Marple's father to pick up his daughter and three other students. His twenty-dollar suit was at the post office. At noon time, the secretary of the trustees counted out only seventeen dollars into Archie Neil's hand—"All we've been able to collect." Archie Neil felt shabby. He really needed that suit. And his shoes were getting bad, too.

John Marple, when he arrived, sensed that something was wrong when he came in. "Just how much did the secretary give you?" John Marple wanted to know. Archie Neil told him. "Well—!" John Marple took out a cheque from his pocket, a creamery cheque, endorsed it, and gave it to Archie Neil. It was for thirty-five dollars. "I'll get the trustees to pay me back," he said. "We'll find it. Time for some quarter dances. Maybe a box social. Anyway, Merry Christmas, Archie Neil."

CHAPTER 23

When did electrical power come to Margaree? To the best of my memory, it was 1939. I have a reason to remember that year.

I was getting out of a truck, and going to walk in to my uncle's place where I was boarding. I was teaching at Margaree Harbour in 1939. It was a Sunday afternoon. It was a big truck. As I was getting out of the truck—I was just using a cane—the gentleman who was driving was in a hurry. He started to leave, and I didn't realize I had stepped out on one of the power poles that they were getting ready to put up. They were lying by the side of the road.

I tripped, and the truck driver didn't realize I fell under the truck. The truck went over me.

I was taken to Chéticamp hospital. My people were called because my kneecap was totally crushed—the left leg (the one that was worse with polio)—and I was very badly smashed inside.

They did not expect me to live. I was in the hospital three days before I was stable enough for them to set the leg. They could not move me, and the leg had to be set right there in the bed. Dr. Doucet's kindness I will never forget.

His bedside manner—brusque, humorous—was to help distract me, but I was too sick to appreciate it at the time.

They put a cone over my face, for the ether. There was a sister, a nun, on each side of me, holding my arms down, to keep me still. I had developed strong arms—because I depended on my arms for everything, even to stand up: lifting myself, using crutches, a cane, playing the violin—I was well muscled. I can't remember who gave me ether. I was afraid of it because somebody told me that while you were going under, you might swear, and my vocabulary wasn't all fit for the ears of nuns. I was worried. I don't know if I actually said anything. But later I found out that just as I was going under, I took with one hand one of the nuns, like she was the weight of a pillow, and flung her over the bed towards where the other sister was. She was not pleased with Dr. Doucet who, though all masked up, let out a big laugh at her expression of astonishment at flying through the air so suddenly.

When I was safely asleep, the leg was set, and I was unaware of my feat of strength.

Regardless of facilities anywhere, nobody could have gotten better treatment than I did at the Chéticamp hospital.

When I awoke, my leg was in a sling about a foot and a half off the bed. I had no idea of dying. It was others who were spreading the report that "Archie Neil is on his last."

My brother Angus was warden at the Highlands National Park at the time. He got a call from home that I had been in an accident and that I had internal injuries and a deep gash on my head, and my leg was smashed. It was the internal injuries that they figured would do me in. Angus was in shaky condition over this because we had played fiddle together, we had gone to dances together, we had done everything in catalogue of good and a lot of bad together. He was feeling miserable that I was dying.

149

Angus had bought a new Chev coupe, a big, heavy power- ful car for the time. But he did not want to go over the mountain alone on the gravel roads. Not that he had any physical fear, but his nerves were in bad shape. He figured he needed company for the trip.

The man who went with him was a great friend of mine and of Angus—Jack Sam Hinkley. He ran a lovely rooming house and dining room just as you come into Pleasant Bay from Chéticamp. Jack would never refuse a favour to anyone. He possessed a great sense of humour.

They started over the mountain from Pleasant Bay towards Chéticamp. All the people who lived on the mountain from Pleasant Bay to Chéticamp had been given new homes by the government because their own land was expropriated for the National Park a few years before. There was only one house left, to the right hand side of the road, down in a deep gully. There were one or two people living there. That day they had a washing hung on the line, including a white sheet. Jack Sam was hanging on for dear life in the pas- senger seat of the car, while Angus was going so fast that the rear end was swinging on the gravel around some of the turns. He was making it, but the faster he was going, the more Jack Sam was praying and preparing for the hereafter. He didn't say a word to interfere with Angus's driving. But just as they rounded a curve, and the car gave an extra sweep, scattering gravel down over the hill, Jack looked down and saw the sheet on the clothesline.

He said mildly, nodding his head at the white sheet, "An- gus, for God's sake, take it easy. They just surrendered!"

CHAPTER 24

Archie Neil was seeing Nora Embree. They considered themselves engaged. The decision had been made only weeks before the accident. She did not like drinking and he had promised to quit, and for the four months before the engagement had had only one drink, as far as she knew. Actually, he'd had a hoot one weekend when she was away, but that did not count so long as nobody told her. And Archie Neil was pretty good at planning his binges. Still, she came to the hospital suspicious, wondering whether he had been drinking when he fell on the power poles, ending up under the truck. He was able to tell her truthfully that liquor had nothing to do with it, unless the fellows who left the poles beside the road were drunk.

Frank Snow landed in the bed next to Archie Neil, his back injured in a collision with a bulldozer working on highway construction. He, too, was strapped down, and for the first few days, they were able to get only glimpses of one another; but they joked to the ceiling about the tyranny of Sister Adultrude, whom they called "The Patron Saint of Purgatory." The truth was that the sister was as smart as she was formidable, and they both enjoyed her conversation. She had lived in Chicago before she joined Filles de Jesus, and was far more worldly than any nun they knew in Cape Breton.

There was a plaster figure of a saint on Archie Neil's bed table that he thought resembled Sister Adultrude. She was an

151

odd saint, he thought, whoever the plaster lady was, with keys attached to the belt of her flowing robes. She was holding a candle, and there was a sheep next to her. The expression of the saint was very grim and ascetic.

Most of the visitors were family. Nora came about once a day. And sometimes a visitor would be good enough to give him a little drink. One evening Angus Y. MacLellan, the light-keeper on Margaree Island, argued his way into a short after-hours visit with Archie Neil.

"With all due respect and by the good grace of the Holy Mother," he told the sister, "I rowed clear from Margaree Island today to see this friend, and against the tide too, and now you're turning me away?"

In exasperation, he told her in Gaelic exactly what he thought, which Archie Neil was happy that the sister could not understand.

But she understood the tone well enough.

"Row yourself back and come again," she told him, "at a civilized time." Then she just walked away. She gave Angus Y. only five minutes, but long enough for him to leave a pint of whiskey. Despite all the pain killers, Archie Neil was grateful for this. This would help him sleep.

"Frank, do you take a drink now and then?"

"I would give anything in the world for a drink right now."

"I'm going to have a little swig first, and give you a go at it."

Neither one of them could move from their beds, or even to get up on an elbow. Archie Neil considered this difficulty as he took a long, deep swallow. He recapped the bottle and wrapped it in a towel.

"Catch it," he instructed, as he raised his shoulders as high as he could and tossed it toward the center of Frank's bed. It landed on him and he grabbed it, had a good drink and threw it back.

"Maybe you should have drunk half and then threw it," Frank suggested.

"We could miss. You drink half of that and you might not be able to throw it."

"But you could have had it first. You wouldn't miss."

"Ah," said Archie Neil, "my reputation precedes me."

There were several more pitches back and forth and they talked about how baseball was probably their true calling. When Archie Neil decided that they should save some for the next day, there was still about a third left in the bottle. But where to hide it. Archie Neil lifted the statue of the saint. It was hollow. Perfect.

When the sister came to check on him about ten o'clock, she commented on his good colour. "We are doing something right for you here."

Next morning, after breakfast, Archie Neil thought it was time for another drink. But when he raised the statue, the pint was gone.

It would be years later before Sister Adultrude would have an opportunity to tell him the truth. The sisters had given the whiskey to a man down the hall, a teaspoonful at a time through the night, to help him through the D.T.'s.

From the hospital, Archie Neil went home to Margaree Forks. He had nowhere else to go. He went home, still encumbered by the unwieldy casts on both feet, using double crutches. He tried to be an appreciative patient but, finally, despite Momma's meals and fussing and Papa's company and conversation, it was all the constraints of home. He chafed under the dependence like a prisoner. He was restless and could think of no escape. And he did not have one red cent. His life felt dried and withered, a desert with no possibility of a drink for endless days and nights.

153

CHAPTER 25

Years later, after I had quit drinking, I was asked by Fr. Webb to go down to Talbot House (an alcohol rehabilitation centre) and tell my story. I went down. And the Sunday I got down there he told me, "I've got quite a crowd in," he said, "and you're not going to probably enjoy talking to them, because a lot of them are badly hung over and in bad shape." I figured that my subject, at my age, could be: You can always make a comeback. Because I was almost sixty when I graduated from college. 1967. I went every Saturday for five years. I drove from here to Antigonish. And I spent all my summers there, all summer. And I got both degrees the same day—Bachelor of Education and Bachelor of Arts. They made quite a fuss about it at the time. Even *Time* magazine had an article about it.

So this was the subject that I was supposed to tell them at Talbot House. They were just sitting down, very dour, and all this sort of thing. I told them, "You people figure that you're feeling very miserable. And you are. I know it. I went through it all. There's not one of you any sicker than I was the day I quit. But," I said, "none of you were arrested for riding in a wheelbarrow, or very nearly arrested."

And I could see their heads coming up as much as to say, This is Cape Breton's outstanding liar.

And I told them a true story. I said, "This is true, whether you believe it or not." I said, "When they used to sell these jugs of wine, Catawba Wine, for two dollars a gallon. There were a couple of sets of boxing gloves in each jug. I went to Inverness and I had four dollars. And I got two jugs of wine. I came back on the truck that takes the mail down to Margaree. I got off at Margaree Forks about ten o'clock at night, and put the two jugs on the side of the road. And I figured to myself, I'm a mile from home. I was sitting there wondering. I said, Somebody will come along.

"And I heard this fellow walking down the road, and I spoke to him. It turned out to be a young fellow quite a bit my junior. And he said, 'I'll tell you what we'll do.' He had a couple of drinks. It was like Bobby Burns and Souter Johnny. We had a few drinks. And he was becoming more active.

"He said, 'I'll tell you, I'll take the jugs and we'll walk the mile down to your place, and we can rest every now and again, if your legs are tired.'

"We only went about a hundred yards and he decided we'll have another drink. We did. All of a sudden he was inspired. There was a group of nuns at Margaree Forks and they had a little barn and a farm, and we were right across the road from the barn. He said, 'I got it. I'm going to steal the wheelbarrow from the nuns.'

"He stole the wheelbarrow and he came down and we put the two jugs of wine in the wheelbarrow, and we were walking like this. We came down to the bridge at Margaree Forks. As the wine was taking hold, he was getting stronger. He became a potential MacAskill suddenly. And he said, 'You can get in the wheelbarrow, and we'll come home like that.'

"We started down, and we were meeting cars. I'm not exaggerating or anything like that. I met one particular car. And when they saw the wheelbarrow, and me sitting in it, and this fellow hauling me home like that, they just ditched her! Went right into the ditch on the other side.

"Everything was going good. Cars were meeting us, were giving us a wide coverage. Until suddenly this car, a fellow slammed on his brakes, and I felt a flashlight right in my face. And here was the constable from Chéticamp. He recognized me. And he said, 'What are you doing there?'— and the wine was right there. I said, 'I'm taking these home.' And he started to laugh. He couldn't stop. He said, 'Look, I'm giving you five minutes and I'll be back. And if you're on the road, I'm going to arrest the two of you.'

"Never touched the wine.

"The fellow ran all the rest of the way home, with me, and I wasn't too light at the time. And we made the gate there at our place just as the constable went down!"

But I embellished it quite a bit when I was telling them. And the first thing, they were just roaring and laughing. And Fr. Webb said he didn't know how in blazes I had done it, but he said, "I laughed myself till I was sick when I heard the story."

And it was true. Actually true.

CHAPTER 26

He went to Nora's in a borrowed car after school. Spring of 1942. The war was on, but Archie Neil was fighting his own battles on the home front. He had thought he was winning, but Nora was not glad to see him. When he came to the screen door, she came out quickly, closing the door behind her after a glance inside.

"Mother is napping."

He had had to find out afterward just who Nora had left with after the dance in Judique. That was three days ago. It had been nearly three months as far as anyone knew since he had had a drink, and Nora had said she would definitely marry him.

Then he had abandoned her at the dance, first drifting away for a chance at someone else's bottle, then afraid after a couple of drinks to go near her. He had kept drinking, did not really know whether or when she left, and then was stupid enough to call her the next day, still drunk, unable to tell her where he was or who was with him, because he really did not know. He said he was sorry and made some excuse, but ended up really angry with her. She told him she left with Mark Strickland. He started to give her hell and she had hung up the phone. Even today, he was still sick.

He had been able to teach school but he ended the last class early. All day he was consumed with thirst, made frequent trips to the water bucket, but the thirst never left him. And he felt fevered. Was it because he drank or because he didn't drink? He would suddenly sweat profusely, and felt waves of almost intolerable edginess. A dropped pencil or a student's whispering annoyed him beyond all bounds. He blew up for an instant when he discovered that one of his eighth graders had not done her homework. Then he was apologetic, spoke more kindly to her, but he felt his tension spreading through the room. After the noon recess, he knew that it was best that they work on assigned essays while he corrected papers. The afternoon dragged endlessly. And the thirst.

Archie Neil decided he must be coming down with something.

Nora took him out on the back patio. He followed her, leaning heavily on his cane, for his legs were not as dependable as they were before the accident three years earlier. He noticed that there were spots on the front of his shirt. He hastily buttoned his jacket. He had eaten several mints to cover his breath. Carefully, stiffly, he sat down on a bench on the patio.

She was beautiful without make-up, and her thick dark hair looked damp and softly tangled as if she had just washed it. She looked younger than she was, and it made him hold back his angry words. They argued often and bitterly these days.

She stooped to pick up an empty seed packet, and stood there folding the paper into a fan shape over and over. "Sorry," she said with a faint smile. She had no idea for what. Then she said, "I planted my Victory Garden this morning." She gathered her hair into a loose knot behind. She avoided looking at him.

"You lied to me," he began.

"Yes, I did." She threw down the folded packet and took a deep breath. "Yes. I felt badly about it after. But you made me so angry. Did you think I wouldn't notice you were drinking? I left with Mark because it was just easier."

"But you're not engaged to Mark. I may be old-fashioned, but I thought engaged women didn't date other men, and then lie about it." The anger and hurt welled up again. He knew he had no right to it, but there it was.

"I should get you a cup of coffee," she observed. "I think you are hung over. Or maybe still drunk."

"I am neither," he snapped.

"Obviously you don't know what you look like," she said. "Or how you smell."

"I don't want to offend you," he said, leaning on his cane to stand.

"Yes, why don't you go home, Archie Neil."

Now he had to get up. He struggled to his feet. He had not wanted it to go like this. He was furious. He lost his balance, and dropped down on the bench. He started to get up again but she put her hand on his shoulder and kept him down.

"No. I don't want you to go. I want you to listen."

"Maybe I don't want to listen to you, Nora."

"I'm going to say it anyway. What a waste you are. A man with talent and intelligence and good looks. A man who can make people laugh and love him. What makes you want to destroy that? I just can't understand it. I thought I could help you, but I can't."

"God, so that's it. I'm one of your causes."

She paid no attention to that.

"What if I were the one who got drunk? Do you want a woman who drinks as much as you do?"

"I never claimed sainthood."

She laughed, but there was no joy in it. "Listen, Saint Archie. I don't care what you think everybody else does. When you're drinking, I feel like I'm crouching in a trench, waiting for the next attack."

"Your comparison is just a little excessive," he said. "I haven't dropped a bomb on anybody for at least a week."

She twisted off the engagement ring and put it in his unresponsive hand, closing his fingers over it.

"I'm all mixed up about us." She smoothed the hair on his temple. He liked the touch.

"There's so much to love in you, Archie Neil. God, I love you. But some of these things make me crazy."

She was quiet a very long time.

He looked at her face, partially hidden by her hair. He noticed the delicate shape of her ear, the tiny earring. He was filled with tenderness and remorse. He had not quite meant what he said. Well, he did mean it, but she was the one who had stung him to it.

She could not have imagined what he was thinking. She decided it was time to talk.

"I lied to you about other things. My father isn't dead; he is an alcoholic. Our family were his prisoners of war. I don't know how my mother thinks because she freezes up when I try to talk about it. I used to hide in the back of my closet when he came home until I knew whether or not he was drunk. I ran there and hid when they argued. And *he* felt like a martyr in his life. All the drama of it. Centre stage. And we had no choice but to act it out with him."

Nora glanced at the house to be sure that her mother was not at the door.

"He broke my arm one night. Momma told people I fell. After, he took us away on a holiday. We all pretended everything was all right then. We were all such good liars. Momma and I even lied to each other. There were worse things too—" She stopped herself from saying more. Then she added, "He didn't die of a heart attack. He just walked away from us one day. He took all the savings and disappeared.

"People thought my mother was the problem. Outside the house, he was everybody's best friend." After a pause, "I hope I never see him again."

Nora was crying now. She took hold of Archie Neil's hand again. She looked at him directly and said, "I'm not as strong as my mother was."

Archie Neil couldn't decide whether to tell her about his family. He remembered Momma's fright when Papa came home after drinking too much. It was a rare thing, but still Archie Neil had not wanted to see it. He had a faint memory of his father's terrible temper, or that he'd been told of times when Papa had done something in a drunken fight—but either it had never been made explicit, or he had blocked out the details.

After one of these episodes, Angus and Archie Neil got into a row with Willie D. They were all very young, but the memory of it stuck. Willie D. said that there were stronger men than Papa at the Forks. Men that could thrash him good if they wanted to. Angus and Archie Neil resented the very thought, and they won the argument by throwing stones at their older brother who retreated laughing. None of the children had seen Papa be anything but respectful toward Momma, even in the face of occasional biting remarks.

The children tended to take sides with Papa.

"Why didn't you tell me a long time ago, Nora?" Archie Neil spoke gently. "If I had known these things —"

"And what would you have done? I don't want to be the person you stop drinking for. I don't want that responsibility."

"I'm not an alcoholic, Nora. I can stop."

"So could my father." She looked at the neat rows of her garden. "I wasn't going to bother with cabbage, but there is room for a row."

"Your father is not me," he said, sensing that she had already left him. "Only a savage would hurt his family like that."

"You already have hurt people, Archie Neil. Your family. Me. Not like my father. But in other ways. And don't tell me that you didn't mean to. Neither did my father."

"What can I do to convince you?"

"I don't want to be convinced."

"I will never take another drink." He said it like a vow.

He tried to give her back the engagement ring, but she would not take it. "Keep it for me," she said, steadily. "I need time to think about whether or not I want to marry. A year."

When he left she was absorbed in preparing a row for the cabbages.

CHAPTER 27

Five dry months later, Archie Neil was relishing life as he seldom had before. He wondered what it would be like feeling like this all the time. He was seeing Nora and the engagement was definitely on, although she hadn't taken back the ring. She said she'd rather wait for the wedding. Still, word had gotten around, and about the only boring thing in his life was the interminable advice about reformed drinkers and the teasing from fools.

It wasn't whether the violin was any good but was the fiddler in tune. And would he play better drunk or sober?

Most people knew that it was not easy, and just left him alone.

One friend whose religion was Alcoholics Anonymous told him that being dry was like always walking on the edge of a chasm, and he said it in a hushed, frankly frightened voice. Archie Neil listened because he loved this man—they had shared more than one blanket on more than one floor—but he considered this the "scared to sobriety" method.

Archie Neil had his own method and it was working. He kept his eye on new clothes and being able to pay for a life with Nora. Besides, thank God, he wasn't an alchoholic.

Archie Neil was pleased with himself. He liked to be alone with Nora. He liked her kisses and he liked her laughter. And it gratified him to know that he'd won her trust.

Still, there were times he felt badly off center, in real pain,

162

and he wobbled on the brink of that chasm, his legs ready to betray him.

When Archie Neil arrived at Archie Dan MacIsaac's, he was greeted by his son Danny.

"Somebody said you might not come."

"No one trusts you when you're sober," Archie Neil joked.

"I've been practicing some new tunes, let's try them out."

"Sounds good."

They sat on the back porch awhile, picking out the new tunes together, holding the fiddles like a ukelele. The tunes drew Ronald Kennedy, a terrific fiddler.

Archie Neil watched the arriving guests. He wondered how many of the cars had liquor in the trunk. There certainly would be some. He regretted having told so many people that he was on the wagon; everybody would be keeping an eye on him, see how quick he'd fall. If he chose, he could have a drink. If he had just one, and ate something after, no one could detect it. Nora need not know.

Someone stopped for a second to lean in and let them know they were crazy as a bag of hammers, and Archie Neil told him he thought he knew that tune. They all laughed. Archie Neil caught the sweet smell of whisky on the joker's breath. He was still feeling like hell, as he had all day. Shaky and fevered. Everything bothered him, the edginess had not abated. It was an edginess that was not exciting; it was an edginess in which he yawned, felt it hard to concentrate on anything, sometimes hard to breathe. He took polite interest in the conversations. But he scarcely paid attention to what he was saying himself.

No! He got up and went inside, to get away. It had nearly driven him crazy to say no when Colin offered him a little bottle, free. But he had said no.

He looked for Nora. She was in the kitchen with other women preparing the food. He watched her a few minutes from the doorway. She looked tasty in a neat flowered dress with a white lace collar. He liked watching her, the careful, precise placement of food on trays, thinking that now he understood her. She laughed easily in her talk with the other women. But he knew what she had been through. And he believed he needed her strength in his life.

Archie Neil captured her on the way by, putting his hand against her waist. She felt delicious, comfortable. And how he needed her assurance and comfort now! She gave him a quick, naughty smile, then made a show of escaping in front of the women.

"Mmm-m, I like your aftershave."

"Mmm-m, I like your lipstick," he whispered back. She slid out of reach.

He turned and saw his cousin Angus MacLennan sitting near the door. He was anxious to avoid him because he had not paid back a loan. Actually, it was complicated. Archie Neil needed a $100 bank loan to cover some overdue debts, but after he secured the loan, he spent it on drink. Then he persuaded Angus MacLennan to co-sign a loan at another bank. But that money was spent and now he owed a total of $300 and he did not have it. And now Angus had seen him.

"Hulloo," he said to Angus.

"I heard you're engaged. Congratulations." Angus did not know that Nora was not actually wearing Archie Neil's ring.

"I think it's an epidemic, Angus. The newspaper's full of it. Another wartime casualty list."

"We might as well catch it and be done." Then: "How's Nora going to handle your problem?" Angus startled him. He was rarely this blunt.

"What problem?"

"The booze."

"I'm handling it fine myself."

"Uh-huh. Don't worry about the hundred bucks. I know you're good for it eventually. Good luck with Nora."

Angus walked away from him.

"Time for action on the homefront, boys!" Archie Neil picked up his fiddle and Danny joined him. He played against the sombre mood in his heart.

There was room enough on the floor for two square sets, and pairs quickly assembled. Archie Neil watched Mark Strickland single out Nora. Strickland ran a successful farm and had the reputation of being a hard worker. He was also well-liked, quiet, genial. Archie Neil would have liked to run him over with a truck. The surge of jealousy was so strong that it surprised him. He drove down into the music. Nora was a good dancer, and he deliberately told himself that he shouldn't mind. But he did mind.

He and Danny played several more tunes, but Archie Neil's playing was off, his hands were sweaty and shaky. He was impatient, he couldn't seem to keep the tempo. He asked Ronald Kennedy to take over for him, told him that he wasn't feeling well.

CHAPTER 28

Archie Neil went outside into the cooler night air. It was almost cold, October, and there had been heavy frosts. He shivered with sweat. The trunks of cars were up and he could see men enjoying themselves, travelling from car to car. It wasn't goddamned fair. Bandy-legged Peter began to sing "Mother Machree." He'd obviously had a few. "I love the dear silver that shines in your hair, And the brow that's all furrowed and wrinkled with care. I'll kiss —"

"Kiss me arse," somebody shouted at him. Everybody laughed.

Allie Delaney was sitting in his car. Allie would be good for a drink. "Can't give you any, Archie Neil," he chided cheerfully. "Don't want to mess with nobody on the holy wagon."

"We'll all be saints together if you don't share the holy water," Archie Neil came back. "You can watch if you like. One drink."

"Bad, eh?" Allie knew the feeling.

"Terrible." Archie Neil held onto the side of the car and leaned on his cane. He was terrified by the ferocity of his craving.

The drink warmed him. The cold air wouldn't bother him now. Allie firmly took back the bottle and wasn't happy when two men offered Archie Neil more.

"Go ahead, we won't tell Nora." So he had several drinks—long, hard swallows. Raw. He thanked them with tears in his eyes. They were dear, kind friends, the best. He loved them. They joked and laughed with the abandon of truant schoolboys. Then most of them went back to the party. Before he left him, Allie told him to stay out of trouble, whatever that meant. Archie Neil didn't dare go in now, not with Nora there.

He sat alone on the tailgate of a truck and smoked several cigarettes, thinking all the time about the open trunk of the car ahead of him. It was Billy Martin's car. When they were drinking together—this was years ago—Billy stole Archie Neil's Highland Whiskey, and then sold it back to him, thinking Archie Neil was too drunk to know. Now he figured Billy owed him a bottle, and he did the proper thing, took one from the trunk and started drinking it. Billy was like that, he thought. A lot of people were like that. Pals on payday and they got him drunk and got him to spend all his money, then he didn't have a damn cent until the next payday unless he played fiddle or borrowed and they wouldn't lend him any. And girls got money from him too, and maybe did him favours, and loans that were never repaid, and how was he going to ask for that back. He decided that's the kind of person he was, he wouldn't ask. He finished Billy's bottle.

Archie Neil stayed where he fell on the lawn. It was very dark. He couldn't seem to get himself oriented. He wasn't sure his eyes were open. He wondered from which direction the bomb would fall. The music had stopped and men had come outside again, but they seemed far away.

He didn't have the strength to yell. He felt chilled again; there was a slight fall of snow; a wind blew from the ocean. He was in his shirtsleeves, having left his jacket inside or on the car, and he wanted his jacket but he couldn't remember exactly where he left it. Maybe inside. But Nora would see him. He was trying to get into one of the cars, but the roll of the lawn had swallowed him. He kept poking around with his cane, trying to touch something, trying to get his bearings.

Danny appeared over him. "I wondered where you went."

Archie Neil said, "Okay," much too loud.

Two men hoisted him to his feet with a laugh and nearly carried him over to sit leaning against a railing, his feet and cane dragging.

"Eisenhower can use a man like me. A man that's risen." He was shivering and Danny offered him his jacket. Danny and Allie struggled to get the jacket on him

"Can't get it in. The man's too big. Can't get it in."

"Aw now don't get dirty," Allie laughed. "Not in front of us young ones."

"I never tell a dirty joke in front of boys," Archie Neil said. "Boys, turn your backs . But youse shou' hear this story, about Peter Dan...." For some reason, Archie Neil figured he wanted to punch Peter Dan, but he couldn't remember why. "A true story."

"You're lying, as usual," Peter Dan laughed. "But go ahead."

"Remember the wake over Smith's last year? You know, at the house up the hill near the South West Margaree Church, back of the cemetery? Well, Ole Peter never made it to pay respects. He got his moonshine in Inverness—and by the time he hitched back to the South West, he was lit—but the sun wasn't. Who's got a cigarette? Whoo—it was dark, dark. Did I fall? Peter wanted to take a leak before he went into the house."

Archie Neil laughed so comically that they all laughed with him. About all that held him up was the men leaning in for the story.

"Course, it just couldn't be avoided. Peter Dan fell into the hole he was peein' in—the grave of the man he'd come to wake." Archie Neil paused for them to laugh. Some of them did. "After he was all petered out, so to speak—" He looked at Danny and Allie frantically. "Whoo—youse boys get me over side of the house. Gotta go myself."

Archie Neil leaned against the side of the building. They turned him around with his face squashed against the shingles. He urinated against the wall, still talking. "Little scar on his forehead? Peter, show 'em. Where he hit his head on a rock in the grave. Out cold." Archie Neil pushed away from the wall, turned, and slammed back against the building, the men's hands keeping him in place.

"Musta thought he went to Hell where he belongs," Allie said. Archie Neil wasn't sure if Allie meant him or Peter Dan.

"No-o. But he got scare of hish life." Archie Neil tried to fix his thoughts on the story. He waxed happily dramatic, swinging out an arm and smacking one of the listeners. "Opened his eyes. Whoo—sun shining through trees, birds shinging, the church music drifting in the air. The funeral's on. He looked up. Got up. Peeked out over the edge of the grave. All he saw—headstones all around. Headstones, all around. 'Jesus!' Peter Dan said, 'this is the Day of Judgement, and God— I'm the first one risen!'" And Archie Neil slapped someone on the chest in appreciation of his own brilliant punch line.

Archie Neil could hear Ronald Kennedy striking up a fiddle tune.

"Whoo—I havta go back in and play tune," he said, trying to walk. They wouldn't let him move. "Promised Archie Dan— Going to throw up." He tried to hold it back. "Get away from me," he warned as Allie approached.

"You want Nora to see you like this?" Allie asked. Archie Neil struggled, but they wouldn't let go of him. Allie and Danny.

"Danny, get away from me." He was furious, shaking them off. "I can take care of myself."

He stumbled out into the windy darkness, ran into a tree, grabbed ahold of it and puked. When he was finished, there were still the dry heaves. He let them bring him home after that, too sick to care.

Later, he told people who asked that he was glad to be a bachelor. He was free. Only himself to worry about. He could come and go as he pleased. All married men managed to talk about is the cost of lumber and the cost of groceries. Married men often looked at him with envy.

He went to Nora and Mark's wedding, and when he congratulated her, he was sincere. He told himself that he narrowly escaped that time, and that it was a good thing.

CHAPTER 29

I got word of Papa's death while I was correcting student papers at Belle Côte. I was boarding with Bill and Mary Matheson. They came to my room and I knew what they were going to tell me. It was strange but earlier a group of friends came by to ask me to play at a wedding, and I said, "No, my father is sick, and I don't think I should go." But I didn't know he was so close to the end.

The first thought I had when I stood at the foot of Papa's bed was that I had disappointed him, and now there was no way to change that.

After the prayers at the gravesite, Father Cormier held Momma's hands and looked directly into her face. She was blind now, and deaf. He knew that she had not heard a word of the church service. He spoke very loud, in part saying, "Cridhe glan soluis am broilleach a leine." He had carefully learned and rehearsed the old saying especially for her. "He had a pure heart of light in the bosom of his shirt."

What made me cry was being a disappointment to Papa. I knew what he wanted for me, and instead of doing something about it, I got to the point where I used to come home in pretty bad shape at times.

Now this is as it actually happened.

One particular night a friend of mine and I were driving home, and he dropped me off at my house. And I managed to get into the house all right. But the next day I met him, and he asked me a rather strange question. He asked me, "Who was the chap who walked in from the gate to the front door of your house last night?"

I laughed at him, because I figured he was putting me on. And he described a man—tall, and dressed in a certain way—which immediately struck me as being the identical image of my father, who was then dead, had passed away. I figured that possibly he was just making this up.

But on three different occasions other people had told me that they were seeing this particular man walking with me whenever I would leave a car. And it was particularly in the wintertime.

So one night I came into my own house, and my two brothers were in the living room. One of my brothers opened the door for me, and looked over my shoulder, and didn't say anything. But the next morning he told me that my father had followed me in to the door, that he was positive that he recognized him. This I again assumed to be a ploy to try to scare me into not drinking any more.

But time went on, a year or so after that. I was at a dance, a place called Chéticamp. And we left Chéticamp in a very bad storm. And I got home to my own driveway. I got out of the car. I started in to the house, home. My last recollection was of sort of falling down in the snow. And I made no attempt whatsoever to get up.

But somehow during the night my brother woke up, and he woke his wife up, and he said, "Archie Neil is someplace out there." And he came out, and he picked me up. And without his assistance I would have died that night.

I didn't speak very much about it for a couple of days afterward, and then I asked him. I said, "Rod, how is it that you were able to come out and find me at three o'clock in the morning in a snowstorm when you were supposedly sound asleep?"

And he looked at me for a moment, and then he said, "Well, if I tell you, you won't believe me." I said, "Yes, I will." He said, "Our father appeared at the side of my bed and told me that you were out there, and I went out." And he said, "Otherwise, you would have been dead."

So, a few things happening like that made me decide that I was through with drinking....

No, actually, that wasn't it.

What made me decide to drop it was the fact that I was on an Easter safari with a group of people, and I came home to my boarding house. I was boarding at St. Joseph du Moine. I left school on Easter Thursday evening. And that was in the days when they had a full week. I hadn't taken a drink for quite a few weeks. And I decided, I've just got to have it—no more school for seven or eight days.

So I went on a bad one. And I was travelling around with the same guy all the time. We weren't sleeping. We were just going from house to house, bootlegger to bootlegger, liquor store or anything. And I came home and I was broke. I didn't come home—I went to my boarding house—and the man with whom I was boarding said, "Archie Neil, come on in the house. You're in pretty bad shape."

And I said, "I know, Thomas." I said, "I won't. I don't want your wife, Adele, to see me like this."

And Thomas said, "Adele—you have her worried worse than your mother. She sees you going by, and she likes you. And she said you've never done anything in the house, or said anything that was out of the way. You've always managed to get to your room. Come on in. I'll tell you what I'll do. If you will stay home, I'll get you two quarts."

I went up to the house, and I said hello to Adele. I was able to walk, navigating okay with a cane, just a cane. I had dispensed with the crutches in 1927 and started using the cane. And I got that I could walk very well with it. And the idea was to get me off the road. By gosh, he brought the two quarts up to my room. And I said, "I'm broke, Thomas." I said, "I'll pay you when I come out of this."

And I started to drink alone.

I had a couple of bottles of rum, and I was drinking alone in my bedroom. All of a sudden I put my hand in my pocket—they had a little store downstairs, and I was going to get some cigarettes. And I didn't have a cent, not one penny in my pocket. And I thought to myself, Here I am forty-three years old, and I've worked since I was nineteen—and I didn't have the price of a package of cigarettes. And the strangest thing about it was—you may think this is crazy—but I had drunk myself sober rather than drunk. I was drinking, drinking, just all alone, straight out of the bottle. And then all of a sudden this hit me, and I said to myself, "This is it. I'm going to quit."

There was a full quart and a half quart there. And I took the half quart. The window was up, and I threw it out the window, smashed it on the rocks. And Thomas heard the smash, and made for upstairs. He said, "What in the name of God is wrong with you?" I said, "I will never take another drink, Thomas."

And Thomas laughed and said, "I've heard that one before. Well, if you're never going to take another drink, I'm going to take that quart." I said, "No. Leave it there. That's going to be a fight between that quart and me—between us," I said.

And that night—of all the sickness and pain and everything else I went through, that night was the worst I ever went through. You're going to laugh at me and say, "He's making it up." But I'll tell you that that bottle had arms on it. It seemed to reach out to me. And I said to myself, for the first time in my life, I'd say, Archie Neil, you have D. T.'s now—when you see things and all of that. And I was able to rationalize. And I'd do that. I'd just pinch myself— yeah, I'm awake. As there's a Saviour above, I'm telling you the truth.

I'd see snakes. As there's a God above me. There were snakes and everything, and they were coming through the keyhole, and they were getting larger as they were coming through. And I was seeing all sorts of ugly faces around me. Nothing pleasant. The most horrible looking faces. Then when I'd sit up in bed and get my bearings, they seemed to disappear. Then I'd just relax and go back to sleep, and as soon as I would be just dozing asleep, back they'd come again. So I knew it was a figment of the imagination.

I was alone in the room, alone all the time. They would have come up if I had called them. But I was alone in the room. And Mrs. Deveau would come up now and again to see if I wanted a cup of tea or something. She was a lady I'll never forget. I was in this shape that when she brought me a cup of tea I wouldn't take the tea in front of her. I asked her to put it on the chair. When I went to take the tea I couldn't—my hands were shaking that badly I couldn't.

And I stayed in bed for two days. I wouldn't come down. And when the following Monday came, I was ready to go back to teach. It was right on the hill above them. It was a two-room school then. I went to teach.

And about two weeks or three weeks afterwards, I came downstairs one day with the quart. I had broken the half quart out the window, but I left the full one. I came down and I put it on the table. And I said, "Thomas, I've gotten a cheque and I'm going to pay you." So I paid him for the quart that I drank. And I said, "There's the other one, or I'll pay you for that. What'll you do with it, break it?" "No," he said, "I'll keep it." He looked me straight in the eyes. "For the first time in my life," he said, "I'm believing you."

And so, from that day on I never looked back. No, never.

CHAPTER 30

Archie Neil saw her at a dance he played at Vernier School, and he liked her at once.

He thought himself the luckiest man in the world when her brother came to him two weeks later to ask him to tutor his sister—and now Margaret made him feel old, clumsy, struggling for a bridge to get across to her.

She accepted him as her teacher, simple as that. But Archie Neil was determined to get close to Mary Margaret Delaney of Grand Etang. She had been away two years in the sanatorium at Kentville. She was cured, but her schoolwork was far behind.

Margaret had finished only Grade 9, and now wanted to work for a high school certificate. He was not slow in accepting the assignment.

As it happened, Archie Neil was boarding with her uncle, Amedee Delaney. When he returned to Amedee's that first night, he studied himself in the mirror in his room. The image surprised him—an obviously crippled man with white hair. His clothes were well-groomed; he was broad shouldered and not unhandsome. But he looked older than his forty-four years, an age some of his friends had grandchildren. He didn't think he was much of a catch.

She is too much younger, he decided. What would she want with an old crippled man who was apt to die so much sooner than herself? One that made only a few hundred dollars a year, and was an alcoholic? He built up a formidable case against himself. And besides, he was used to the freedom to go where he wanted, when he wanted, to live completely for himself. That might have been enough, except that he felt his life was lightless and hollow.

He learned more about her. She was eighteen years younger, and in Kentville she took bookkeeping and accounting classes, passing with high marks. Her father was Marcellin "Mike" Delaney who worked as a contractor in the woods for the Oxford Paper Company, and her mother was Mary May. They had a large family; he heard there were seventeen children, though some had died young.

In the following weeks, they worked at a small table in the parlour of Amedee's. He found her a quick learner, conscientious. But she was also prim and matter-of-fact, and he either could not get her to be more personal or she simply refused to acknowledge that he was trying. When they met in her father's house, she maintained classroom-like decorum. What he first took as shyness proved to be a lily in wrought iron.

One evening he sat close to her while she laboured over the final scene of Hamlet. He read aloud for her, warming to the passion of Hamlet's dying words: "Give me the cup.... O, I die Horatio.... The rest is silence." He was deeply moved once again when he read Horatio's, "Now cracks the noble heart."

"Ridiculous."

He was taken aback by her scorn for Hamlet and Ophelia, lovers that Margaret considered "foolish." She had no commiseration for dark souls in torment. She liked things steady, clear, practical.

"They deserved it," she commented, satisfied that the whole lot met a just end.

She was ready for math. But that was by far too summary an execution of Shakespeare, especially after Archie Neil's efforts to explain it, to read it dramatically and with all his heart.

"Can't you imagine what it would be like, Margaret?"

"No." She got up to prepare the coffee.

"I mean, to know what is right to do but not be able to make up your mind to do it? Or to be attracted to what you know to be absolutely wrong and not be able to resist it, even though

Wedding, September 4, 1954: (left to right) Angus, Archie Neil, Margaret (Delaney) Chisholm, and Margaret's sister, Mary Helen Delaney

Archie Neil and Margaret's home in 1957

Graduation from St FX University, 1967

Northeast Margaree Consolidated School, February 1971

Margaret holding Robert, and Archie Neil

Correcting student papers

Studio portrait of Archie Neil at CBC Radio recording additional material for "Archie Neil's Cape Breton"

With Margaret and Archie Neil, their children: (left, l. to r.) Michelle, Leona, and Robert; (below, l. to r.) Noreen and Michelle. Michelle is holding her daughter Meghan.

Left: entering the Cape Breton Fiddlers' Association 1989 surprise testimonial banquet in honour of Archie Neil. The surprise worked: Margaret said, "He had gone absolutely white."

Below: Archie Neil with one of his Elderhostel sessions at the Normaway Inn

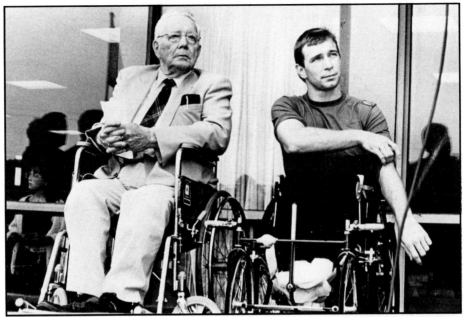

**Archie Neil with Rick Hansen
in Port Hawkesbury during the
"Man in Motion" Tour, 1986**

With granddaughter Meghan

**Margaret and
Archie Neil Chisholm**

you know the results will be disastrous? I think there has to be a little bit of Hamlet and Queen Gertrude and Ophelia in most people."

"Ha."

"Did you know that I am a reformed alcoholic?"

She buttered two tea biscuits, took sugar from the cupboard, glanced at the clock.

"That's none of my business."

"I just thought it would be better for you to hear it from me. People like to tell stories about me."

"I have heard a few. I make up my own mind."

After several more sessions together, he still could not guess in what way she had made up her mind about him. He looked forward to those classes and he missed her as soon as she was gone. She smelled good and had a quick mind and he just liked being with her.

Gradually, he told her about his past, carefully. She listened without comment.

One evening in late spring, they sat on the doorstep for the lessons. It was a gorgeous Inverness County evening, the ocean rich with a dying sun. To stay inside was out of the question. He thought of her now as proud and exacting, but also tempting and close. He put his arm around her shoulders, leaning into a math problem—but she moved away abruptly at his touch.

"Excuse me, Mr. Chisholm, but I don't think my uncle would approve of that—and from a teacher!" He had the sense to know that she was not being coquettish. He found himself mortified, blushing.

"I don't usually kiss students," he laughed, to cover his embarrassment. "I hoped that I could be a little more than a teacher to you, Margaret."

"I think not, Mr. Chisholm."

He tried to ask her questions about herself, but she offered little. Now that she had a little power, she let him know that she did not like his smoking. He refrained from smoking near her, most of the time.

"Oh now, Margaret," he bantered. "You must have some bad habits of your own."

"One of them is I don't like bossy people," she countered. "Or nosey ones either."

"I hope you don't find me totally unlikeable?"

"I won't answer that."

At the beginning of summer, she stopped the classes. He worried that she had heard lies about him black enough to reject him both as a teacher and as a suitor. He did not know which view of things hurt him more. But he was not about to be put off.

Finally, his persistence wore her down. He took her to see a matinee in Chéticamp starring Marilyn Munroe. Margaret found the movie trivial and did not have much to say about it. But during their lunch afterwards, she spoke with vehemence about an elderly neighbour who had just died. He had been taken in by relatives who then neglected him, enjoyed his pension and gave him a pauper's funeral. She spoke of them with such severity, with such a tenacious sense of this injustice, that Archie Neil decided that he deeply admired Margaret, possibly even loved her.

They took a roundabout route home, enjoyed the late afternoon and the long twilight of the summer evening. He spoke at length about teaching and his students. In front of her house, they sat in his car just enjoying the cool air, the evening. He put his arm around her shoulder. She did not move. But his timing was not auspicious. Her father and mother were out for an evening stroll.

"Holy Fright!" said Mr. Delaney. "The teacher, he got his arm around Margaret!"

"My mother had a caller—Hetta McEvoy," Archie Neil told Margaret. "She told Momma I should marry a good Scotch girl, someone my own age."

Margaret was making up a guest list for the wedding. "That's okay, Archie Neil. I was going to tell you about the visit I had from her daughter, Freda. She told me to leave you for someone my own age—and sober."

Everybody seemed to have advice. Her friends found him too old. People remembered Archie Neil as a cripple and a drunk and a rake. They told one another that "Poor Margaret will see more dinner times than dinners. He'll be no good a provider when he's drinking again."

Archie Neil said that he wished he had had time to be a rake.

"Ha," said Margaret—something akin to "nonsense," and "fat chance" and "I'm sure you did your share."

In any case, Margaret had made up her mind, and she sat there serenely and competently making preparations for their wedding.

Archie Neil had never been happier. He told anyone who would listen that he resolved he would be a good provider for Margaret. He played at every dance he could and he put most of the money away. But there was one temptation he could not resist.

He showed up one day with a new Pontiac, fire engine red, a black top and chrome up to the gills. He thought it was exquisite; Margaret considered it conspicuous, even gaudy. She called him a showoff. And he was unrepentant, delighted, and she forgave him quite willingly.

On a hill above the road, about a mile from Archie Neil's old home, was a tiny cabin facing the Margaree River. The view was lovely, a sweep of pasture down to the water. The cabin was owned by Charlie LeBlanc who lived in East Bay. Archie Neil approached him, expecting to pay $1500. He was delighted to be asked for only $400. So Archie Neil had enough money to have the cabin repaired, painted inside and out, and wired. The water system remained a handpump on the veranda, and no plumbing indoors. They bought new furniture, put oilcloth on the floor, and figured it looked like a doll house. It was their own home.

But Archie Neil didn't own the land, and they could be put out of the cabin at any time. Several people had tried to buy the land and the owner, an elderly woman named Mary Chiasson, refused to sell. She lived with her son Peter on another part of the land.

Archie Neil visited Mary and Peter. He tried to seem relaxed, chatty. She just let him talk and talk. Peter sat and watched. Everyone knew why Archie Neil was there and they talked on and on about everything else.

Finally, he asked her to sell the land. Then he kept talking. He talked about Margaret and the wedding and that he never had a house of his own and that the cabin was really transformed now and that they wanted to stay there. And Mary cut him short. She said the land belonged to Peter. "Talk to Peter." So Archie Neil just shifted in his chair and started the story again. And that made Mary laugh.

"You might as well sell it to the son-of-a-gun, Peter. He'll only talk you out of it anyway."

Mary and Peter had made their decision long ago.

In the summer of 1954, Archie Neil saw very little of Margaret. He played at every dance, wedding and festival, to have enough money for their own wedding and a honeymoon. Starting in July, he played for thirty-six dances, thirty-six nights in a row. Later, he joked that he wore out three terrific piano players that summer: Maybelle Chisholm, Josie Ross, and Catherine Rankin. During Old Home Week in Inverness he played at the CMBA Hall, from eleven in the morning till late in the afternoon, and then started up again at eleven that night, playing until three in the morning. Margaret worked at the post office in Grand Etang.

Angus arrived at the cabin the first of September, the night before the wedding. He worked then at the steel plant in Sydney. He came to play the fiddle and to be Archie Neil's best man.

"I'll tell you, Archie Neil," he said. "I promised to be sober for the wedding and I will. But a little one now—"

Angus looked tired. Archie Neil took the whisky from the cupboard and put it on the table in front of Angus.

"How about I fry us up some steaks?"

"Sure," Angus said, abstracted. He took out his violin and opened the door to the veranda. Angus played a few moments of "The Mockingbird." Then he sat in the quiet.

It was half past three in the morning, and the wedding was at nine. They ate their supper, and Angus had several drinks. They drove over to Roddy's and woke him up. Angus and Roddy had drinks and offered Archie Neil a little one, and he enjoyed saying no.

The only difficulty Archie Neil had was to convince Roddy that he should not wake his wife for a waltz in his underwear at five in the morning, even if the great Angus Chisholm were playing the music. He began plying the coffee.

Margaret was dressed in blue. Father Briand said the ceremony at the church at St. Joseph du Moine. The day was marred only by the fact that Momma was too frail to be there; she was now completely deaf and blind. True to his word, Angus was sober.

After the ceremony, the lawn in front of the Delaney house was packed with guests. Through the day they were served breakfast, a luncheon, and a dinner. In the evening, Thomas Deveau chauffeured Archie Neil and Margaret to East Margaree. An open air stage was set up for dancing while Angus Chisholm and Hector MacDougall from Bay St. Lawrence drove the fiddle music, and Maybelle Chisholm played the piano.

Archie Neil was almost unbearably proud. And Margaret was his forever.

CHAPTER 31

They were married only four months when Archie Neil fell. He had come outside on his way to Christmas Eve Mass. Margaret wanted to finish preparations for the ceilidh afterwards and decided to stay home. He was going to pick up members of the choir on the way.

The night was warm and there was wet ice on the back steps. He leaned on the cane, slid, and went down.

X-rays of his leg and hip were diagnosed as a sprain. "It will heal itself."

But it did not heal. He was in constant pain. When he returned to teaching after Christmas, pushing the clutch pedal brought sweat to his face. It was a blustery winter and some days he made it only as far as Margaree Harbour, shaken and white from the torment in his hip. Margaret did not know how to drive, so Joe Cormier had agreed to take him from there through the fields to Belle Côte with his horse and wood sleigh. Then there were still the eight steps to climb at the Belle Côte School.

He wanted the pain to go away. Margaret would mention a doctor and Archie Neil would get surly. His life was just beginning and he suspected that he did not want to know what another doctor would tell him. But he did not want to be immobile again.

Dr. MacIsaac sent him to Dr. Bernard Miller in Halifax. They discovered at their first meeting that they were students together at Saint Francis Xavier in 1925.

"You drove a car like that?" Dr. Miller asked, disbelieving.

Dr. Miller called in Dr. Tom Acker, a bone specialist. He found the hip dislocated, and said that now it was too late to put in a pin, the hip socket had filled in. The only answer would be a fitted caliper and brace. They told Archie Neil that he would suffer.

"We have to set the bone back in place. The pain you have now is not going to go away for quite some time. It might even get worse."

"But I'm going to keep walking?"

"We hope so. Forget the cane, though. You'll need crutches."

There were many trips back to Halifax to fit him for the brace. Archie Neil drove, having learned to push in the clutch with his cane. He worried about the fees, for there was no medical insurance; with the three specialists involved, he was sure the bills would be in the thousands. He worried about work, driving a car, about losing his house and land. The accident kept him from playing violin and he missed that income as well. Margaret was frugal, but their combined savings could not cover anything major. She had the part-time job at the post office in Grand Etang, but the wages were small.

"I'll get a loan to pay you," he assured Dr. Miller, nervous that he would be perceived as not being good for his debts. "I have $500. I can give you that right now and as soon as—"

"I've told you before," Dr. Miller interrupted, "don't worry about that. Tom and Carl and I have agreed that this is a personal project. We are not going to charge you one cent. Now let's see how you do with the brace."

Archie Neil sat there and cried.

He cried again when Dr. Grumdke put the brace on him— this was excruciating pain. The brace held him in a vice from waist to ankle.

Archie Neil laboured to walk with the brace, now forced to lean heavily on two crutches. The German doctor told him, "It will be a fight between you and the brace. I hope you'll be the winner."

Archie Neil returned to teaching the next day, wearing the brace. He fought his way up the eight stairs, damning the brace at every step. The smaller children watched him and one asked why there was water on his face. By the end of the day, he was exhausted and profoundly discouraged.

"Margaret, you'll regret the day you married me," he said, as she propped him with pillows on the chesterfield. "You should have listened to them—'more dinner times than dinners.'"

"We haven't missed any dinners yet."

"I'm the luckiest man alive," he said, taking her slim hand in his own, "to have a wife like you."

She made a grimace. "Shut up."

The next morning, they quarreled. "We went through all this to get that brace." She was furious. "The doctors want you to wear it. So you go and put it on. You are not going to school without it. Why are you giving up after one day? I never thought you were a quitter, Archie Neil."

"I can walk better without it." He left the house, with only his cane and one crutch.

It was true that it was easier to walk without the brace, and the pain was less, but Dr. Acker had explained to him clearly what would happen if he did not wear it: the rapid deterioration of the bones, increasing immobility, decreasing ability to balance. There had been irreversible damage already.

By June, he had made a truce with the brace, and the pain receded, but he had lost mobility and balance. He was in constant danger of falling forward. He was unable to carry anything when he walked. He began to think more about what it had been like, crawling on his belly, to find the normal things of life hopelessly inaccessible. He sensed a closing of doors, a narrowing of his life.

During their first years together, Margaret admitted to only two disappointments: the lack of indoor plumbing, and the fact that she was not yet pregnant, the connection of which was their private joke. After the first year, they got the plumbing. They joked about that for awhile, but they remained childless.

CHAPTER 32

In 1956, Archie Neil ran for public office in Inverness County. He did it for the same reasons he became a Conservative when most Chisholms before him were Liberals—because it was a chance to go contrary, take up the challenge, to take the risk. A moment's thought told him that he did not have as good a reputation as he might have liked to bring to public life. But it was also an opportunity to prove that he had a new life now. Still, running for office was something he was sure he would not have sought had A. R. MacNeil of Inverside and Dan Larry MacFarlane of Broad Cove Marsh, both prominent Conservatives, not come to the Belle Côte schoolhouse asking him to run.

They probably weren't all that certain about Archie Neil themselves. He had seen them from the school window, sitting in their car all morning, possibly getting up the courage to come in and tell him that they both were positive that he would give a good account of himself. Archie Neil reminded them that he still had a past he had not yet lived down.

"If only saints ran elections there wouldn't be any elections." Archie Neil agreed that it was hard to argue with that.

Actually, they were looking for the kind of balance that wins votes. In those days, the winners would represent all of Inverness County, which had not yet been divided into Inverness North and Inverness South. Of the two men elected, it was advisable to have one a Protestant and the other a Catholic. The two Liberal MLAs were Rod MacLean, a Protestant, and J.

Clyde Nunn, a Catholic. So far, the Conservatives had been able to find a Protestant, A. J. Davis, a returned soldier. But they needed a Catholic, and it was a chance to prove himself. Archie Neil could hardly say no.

He quickly suffered many of the indignities of running for public office. First of all, he had to admit that he could not afford it. The party would pay for the substitute teacher while Archie Neil campaigned, plus gasoline, and would give him $200 for living expenses.

The night his candidacy was announced he overheard someone say that "the Tories scraped the bottom of the barrel this time." He promised himself he'd remember that remark when that man came looking for favours after the election. He was already feeling a little like a man in power.

But first, the indignities. He had to crawl in and out of the car dozens of times each day, canvassing from home to home, navigating the stairs and introducing himself and telling people of his intention to run, asking for their vote. They all knew his background, his habits and indiscretions. But they knew he was a committed teacher, and a reliable fiddler. That should be worth something at the polls.

At some houses, the people were put off because he did not give away liquor or even candy bars. Sometimes his welcome was extremely thin. But who could he believe? In Tory homes or Liberal homes, they'd shake his hand and tell him, "You've got my vote" or "I wouldn't do you any harm." He knew his opponents were likely to get the same response. One grandmother in a Liberal family took his hand and patted him on the arm, sympathetic, asking, "Mr. Chisholm, couldn't a fine man like yourself find something better to do? It's so hopeless for you to try to take a Tory vote out of Inverness County."

Still, he made his rounds. He saw Margaret only at breakfast, day after day. He started at eight in the morning and sometimes ended at three the next morning. He'd canvas Pleasant Bay, have a meeting in Chéticamp, and then hurry on to another meeting in Inverness. The meetings at schoolhouses and halls were packed, and by evening he was often exhausted. One night he fell asleep in his chair at a community hall gathering, and the word was out that he was drinking.

But he plugged away at it, visited more homes, dragged poor Margaret along to the meetings. Even Margaret was hard on him. She had not wanted him to run for the office but if he wanted to, okay. But she criticized him as well. One night a speaker told the audience that Archie Neil's brace was paid for by the Canadian Paraplegic Association, that he had taken charity when he could well afford to pay for the brace. Archie Neil *had* received some help, but he handled it badly on stage, ripped into his opponent savagely, told the audience that the accusation was almost a lie, made all his points—and earned Margaret's scorn.

"You showed them what they wanted, Archie Neil. They got you angry."

He finally admitted that she was right. "I am pig-headed." And when they went to bed he asked her whether she was still angry, whether he could sleep with her or should he go out and join the pig. She said "Oink" just before they fell asleep.

But this was Nomination Day in Port Hood, fourteen days before the election, and the people gathered on the lawn of the red brick courthouse expected blood. What they got instead was a kind of class reunion between Archie Neil and his opponent, J. Clyde Nunn. They had seen little of one another since Archie Neil's year at St. FX in 1925, and the crowds looked on with a mix of disappointment and confusion at a Clyde Nunn with a friendly arm slung over Archie Neil's shoulder.

Archie Neil teased Nunn for having unfair advantage in this race, since he was already prominent on radio. Nunn said that Archie Neil surely didn't expect him to give up his announcing career just to be a success in politics. Then he sang part of "Pride of Glencoe" for Archie Neil in the voice of the toothless persona he often pretended to interview on his radio show.

"You know J.," Archie Neil told Nunn, sitting with him on the back of the truck that served as the speaker's platform, "there is a story about when my uncle was running for office, Dr. Chisholm. A great friend of my uncle's yelled out from the crowd, 'Three cheers for Dr. Chisholm'—and the cheers went up. And a Tory standing quite near, he shouted out on maybe the second or third cheer, 'Ah, three cheers for the devil.' And a Liberal replied, 'Okay—you cheer for your man, and I'll cheer for mine.'"

Then he admitted, "You know, this is not going to be easy. That crowd could get vicious."

"We'll handle her, Archie Neil. You know as well as I do, Nomination Day wastes time and money. We'll have fun with it. And it won't change anybody's mind."

Archie Neil wanted to know whether there was truth in the story that Nunn, visiting homes, had once heard an old woman's confession in order to win her vote.

"Where did you hear that?"

"That answer doesn't tell me that it isn't true, Clyde. The story I heard was that you and Rob MacLean arrived at this house. No electricity. About dusk. You both were dressed nicely. Dark three-piece suits, in the fall of the year. And in this house there was this old lady sitting in the corner. Everything clean and fine. You, Clyde, the way I heard it, you were wearing a black homburg hat, black coat, white silk scarf. And the old lady—her eyes were dim, only kerosene lamps. She was saying the rosary. And you looked like a clergyman, like a priest. She spoke Gaelic. And you didn't realize she thought you were a priest. You talked about getting her vote. And she said that she would vote for you if you heard her confession. And to your credit, the story goes that you were in a quandary. Should you listen to her confession to get that vote? And Rob MacLean said, 'Go ahead, hear her confession.' He said, 'If Archie Neil were here, he'd do it.'"

To which Clyde Nunn replied, "And I don't doubt but that you would, Archie Neil."

"That doesn't answer the question, Clyde."

Waiting for speeches to begin, Archie Neil told Nunn that, yes, the story was true about Dr. MacLennan's debate with Hibbert Tupper right here in Port Hood, that they really did put the run on Tupper despite the fact that he held a federal cabinet post at the time.

"Sir John A. called Tupper 'bumptious,'" Archie Neil said. "Good thing, too. He needed bounce that day in Port Hood if he was going to save his hide. You see, Hibbert came in on a yacht—I think it was 1896 or right around there. And when he spoke, people here didn't care what he sailed in on. My uncle's friends heckled him so bad that he turned to Dr. MacLennan on the platform. He said it really low so that nobody else would hear. He said, 'Dr. MacLennan, I wish you would call off your dogs for a few minutes. Give me an opportunity to talk.'

"Well, my uncle was happy to oblige him. He got up and the crowd quieted down a bit, and he said in his best platform voice, 'Sir Tupper has just asked me to call off my dogs.'

"Lots of big Highlanders in the crowd that day. All hell broke loose. And they had to surround Tupper and escort him right down to the boat, or he would have been slaughtered."

Nunn promised that he wouldn't call anybody a dog that day if Archie Neil promised to do the same. They shook hands in front of a miserable crowd, and Archie Neil got up to give his speech.

His fine voice served him well when he offered his opening remarks:

"The Liberals have had power here in Nova Scotia since 1933," Archie Neil began. "Twenty-three years of Liberal government, and Ladies and Gentlemen, look around you. Are we as prosperous as we deserve to be? How many schools, my friends, have been closed? How many communities have been diminished because there are no jobs for our young people? We are losing our best product, our youth, some of our strongest and our smartest citizens, to the more prosperous places. Look around you. Cape Mabou, Foot Cape, Port Ban—dozens of other places in our beautiful Inverness County, deserted now. Where there were families and houses, there are only sheep today. Are the Liberals not like the lairds of Scotland? 'Shame on the tyrants who brought desolation. Who banished the brave and put sheep in their place. Where once ruled a nation, rank weeds have their station.' Open your minds, Ladies and Gentlemen, and see the reality. Who was it that proposed the old age pension? The Conservatives. It was proposed by the Conservatives, who really care about what happens to the good people of Nova Scotia."

Archie Neil sat down, proud of both the jeers and cheers. J. Clyde Nunn stood up to speak.

"Well, it appears that Mr. Chisholm feels that he is speaking to a weedy audience, or perhaps he thinks that we are all sheep—I'm not quite sure which. Anyway, he seems to be suggesting that we are not quite as smart as the people who can be found in other parts of Canada. You know, the ones of us who are still here because we are not smart enough to move away." Nunn paused to give the crowd a chance to laugh and cheer. "Perhaps we ought to blame some of the teachers for not making us smarter."

That delighted the audience, and Nunn had to give them a chance to quiet down.

"Dear Friends," Nunn went on, "a promise is only hot air unless it is carried through. It is not the one who makes the promise who deserves the credit, it is the one who fulfills it. Let us remind Mr. Chisholm of a fact of Nova Scotia history that the good teacher seems to have overlooked. It was the Liberals who were the first to actually *pay* the old age pension!"

J. Clyde Nunn sat down to the roar of the crowd. He and Archie Neil did not talk now, listening while Rod MacLean and A. J. David delivered their remarks.

At one point, Archie Neil reached in his pocket for a cough drop. He reflected that perhaps the agreement about calling off the dogs should have extended to the sheep as well.

"I could use something for my throat too," Nunn said to Archie Neil.

"Certainly," Archie Neil said. He reached in his pocket and handed Nunn his penknife.

Archie Neil lost that election of October, 1956, but he managed to reduce the Liberal majority. Conservative Robert Lorne Stanfield became premier, but in Inverness County the Liberals won. Archie Neil felt he had given them a run for their money, reducing their majority to less than half of what it had been. And he was glad that it was over.

But it wasn't over. Archie Neil was a defeated candidate locally, but with his party in power he discovered that he had considerable say in appointments, public jobs, and pensions. All his tirades against Liberal patronage came back to haunt him with a vengeance. He woke up with the ladle to the patronage trough right in his hand. The stream of people to his door, many of whom insisted that he had their vote, confused and finally overwhelmed him. Conservatives wanted the government trucking jobs, wanted to sell highway machinery, get work on the bridge and road construction, get a pension, have something done for a son or daughter, or just have a half hour to generally complain. Protestants wanted to be sure that he did not forget them when he made his decisions.

Margaret's kettle never cooled after the election. Watching her with the "guests," he felt that she was the better politician. And they still did not seem to have two hours in a row to themselves. There were trips to Halifax to meet with the Minister of Highways or someone from the Department of Health. He got a patronage perk himself, an appointment to the Pensions Board, but that only ate up more time and contributed the equal of two days pay to his $160-a-month teacher's salary. Any way he looked at it, Archie Neil figured he had an extra, full-time and unpaid job.

He held district meetings. He established committees to decide on the disposition of government jobs in each area. He still had to arbitrate in the midst of a lot of bickering, but he was satisfied that most people who received the jobs had local support and would probably do the job well.

When he ran again in the 1960 election, it proved a very close race. His disappointment at losing was balanced by the very narrow margin. After that, Dr. Jim MacLean expressed an interest in the next election, and took over the candidate's work.

Archie Neil had by then chosen other ways to have a public life. It probably started with Denise Kieran's request that he organize a fund-raising campaign for the Canadian National Institute for the Blind in the region from Terre Noire to Gillisdale. He found it continually pushed open the doors his body tried to push closed. He fell again, and then again, and he eventually was confined to a wheelchair. But four decades later he was still campaigning for the blind. And the March of Dimes. The Children's Aid Society. The Canadian Paraplegic Association.

And the list goes on.

CHAPTER 33

Momma died at the age of one hundred, the year before Michelle, the fourth child, was born. She had lived to hold three of Margaret and Archie Neil's children, but she saw and heard only the first-born, Robert Lorne.

"Not a damn thing wrong with his legs," Dr. Jim MacLean had shouted to Archie Neil over the phone. "He's just like his father. All mouth."

Archie Neil and Margaret had been married six years and had given up hope. They had kept a neighbour's baby during the mother's long illness, and when that child returned to her own family, they were left bereft, empty. Then they took in a foster child who was physically handicapped, lavished him with attention but could not overcome his emotional problems, and they could not keep him. And then when Margaret was thirty-five and Archie Neil was fifty-three, Robert Lorne was born, December 6th, 1960, named for the Conservative Premier of Nova Scotia, Robert Lorne Stanfield. Archie Neil would hold the child in the air and say aloud, "This is mine."

Three years later, they were not sure whether Momma knew that she was holding Noreen, born on Momma's birthday, July 11th. When Archie Neil first saw Noreen, her brow drawn into a worried frown, he would smooth the tiny furrows with his finger and say, "Be happy. You'll be all right. Papa loves you."

Momma's hands were busy in those last years, motions something like spinning wool or washing dishes or folding

clothing—but she was blind and deaf and her hands were empty. She was ninety-seven that year. Once, she started to sing
with the little girl in her arms, the faint ghost of "Ba, ba, mo
ghaol"—"Hush, hush, my dear"—then the tune, "Chi mi gun
dail an t-aite 's an d'rugadh mi...." The song faded. Archie Neil
remembered the song as having something to do with "the
place I was born"—but the Gaelic song had faded for him as
well.

When Leona was born a year later in September, they simply placed her for awhile in her grandmother's arms. Leona was
a tiny, delicate infant, more like Margaret than Archie Neil.
Momma did not seem to know that she was holding a child.

Archie Neil and Roddy watched Momma's last hours in the
dim room off the kitchen, the room where her children were
born, where she had been loved by her husband; the room Archie Neil shared with his parents when he was first paralyzed,
the room where Papa had died. The only sounds were the clock,
her ragged breathing, the crackle of the fire in the kitchen
stove. Father Briand was retired now; a close friend, he
watched with them through the night.

Now and then a faint sound came from Momma, and her
hands fluttered up like leaves. Sometimes Archie Neil held her
cold hand for awhile, needing her more than she needed him.
He was sorry for the pain his broken body caused her, and for
the pain his selfishness had caused. He wanted her long hair to
fall over him like a veil, he wanted her familiar scent, he wanted her song and her forgiveness.

Momma's arm was cold now, as cold as her hand. Father
Briand held a crucifix near her. Roddy was on his feet.

"O merciful God," Father Briand prayed, his hand lightly
on Momma's forehead, "O God most kind, grant to thy servant,
Isabel MacLennan Chisholm, a full discharge from her sins.
Renew in her whatsoever has been vitiated by human frailty, or
by the frauds and deceits of the world, and bind her fast as a
member of redemption, to the unity of the body of the Church.
Have compassion, O Lord, on her sighs, have compassion on
her tears, and admit her, who has no hope but in thy mercy of
the sacred gift of thy reconciliation."

Just before dawn, there was a deep intake of breath. She raised her head slightly from the pillow. Later, they would say that her blind eyes looked at someone at the foot of her bed with glad recognition. She tried to say a name. And then she died.

"Momma!" Archie Neil cried out.

Father Briand's face was washed with tears as he gave her absolution. "Go forth, Christian soul, out of this world, in the name of God the Father Almighty.... Mayest thou, our friend and mother Isabel, be placed among the companies of the blessed, and enjoy the sweetness of the contemplation of thy God forever."

PART THREE

Archie Neil's Cape Breton

CHAPTER 34

"Failte. This is Archie Neil speaking from Margaree Forks. Welcome to this land of saints and scholars. And welcome to 'Archie Neil's Cape Breton.' I'm happy you could make it for our regular Wednesday afternoon get-together. Cape Breton is rich in stories—tragic, proud, comic. The stories ultimately come from many cultures—and while the language and details may differ, there is much in common in folklore, a higher culture, a universality. We've rounded up some rousing good tales just for you. You will hear fiddle music from the likes of Buddy MacMaster, Donald Angus Beaton, and Kinnon Beaton, with Betty Lou on the piano.

"Let's start off right with Buddy, a man who doesn't need introduction here. He's come a long way from that first time he played in public at an amateur hour in Port Hood. Now he has a reputation across North America and overseas as one of our best Scottish violinists. Here's Buddy with a medley of Inverness jigs."

Brian Sutcliffe, the program's producer, lit his cigarette and one for Archie Neil, while Buddy played to the microphone. Brian kept an eye on the thick cables running from the recording equipment in the back bedroom, along the narrow hallway and through several chair legs on its way to the table set up in the living room. He watched whenever someone picked their way over the cables on the way to the bathroom, and watched them again walking back with one hand along the wall, working their way to the living room. The cables led to microphones on the table.

All morning Michelle, Noreen, Leona, Robert, and Michelle's husband Gordon Crowley had worked around Archie Neil while he sat in his wheelchair and smoked cigarette after cigarette, already checking out the window for the first arrivals, and talking away. He was up before anyone, dressed in a gray suit and tie, ready hours in advance. The family moved furniture and worked with Margaret in the kitchen, and made calls for Archie Neil as he thought of them, inviting more people.

Now, around the table were the guests who would be telling stories this session: Dan Angus Beaton from Blackstone, Father John Angus Rankin from Glendale, Paddy MacDonald from Inverside, and Jim St. Clair from Mull River. The room was filled with people, standing or clumped on the sofa or padded chairs, one or two in the seat and whoever could fit on the arms. Sound equipment and technicians were jostled by the movement of people between the living room and kitchen.

Each visit, CBC Radio taped enough for several weekly shows called "Archie Neil's Cape Breton"—and every session was a party. It was the risk Brian and Archie Neil wanted to take: Get the show out of the studio, try to capture some of the life of a real Cape Breton ceilidh.

"After all," Archie Neil told him when they first discussed the program, "stories are told best where they mean the most"—at home, in the living room or kitchen, surrounded by friends.

Today, the taping had begun but storytellers and musicians were still arriving through the back door, along with relatives and friends who could not be kept away. They knew the door would be open at Archie Neil and Margaret's. It was difficult to keep people quiet during the tapings, though they were pretty respectful when Brian gave the signal that the tape was rolling. Despite the wires and microphones, it was a real ceilidh. CBC Radio had even donated enough liquid refreshment to help keep the mood mellow.

Archie Neil enjoyed inviting each visitor to have a drink. "There's plenty," he said, "comes right out of your taxes. You'll pay for it anyway." Even after all these years, it was still a test for him, it was still a matter of pride.

"That was a good clip, Buddy," Brian commented when the tape was off. He accepted a cup of Margaret's tea and a sandwich, and remarked to her that he didn't know how she managed to find room to do anything with so many bodies in the way. But she was too busy to chat.

Hector MacDonald arrived. Margaret took his coat in the kitchen, and he came into the living room, chapped hands reddened with cold. He was a large man, a miner and woodsworker. "She's cold in Broad Cove, bye," he said, scrunching down on a short stool next to Archie Neil.

"How cold is it?" Archie Neil asked.

"So cold a boiling kettle would freeze over a roaring fire."

"God, that's bad, " Brian said, laughing along with the others who were close enough to hear. By now there were five conversations going on in the room. He crouched down. "I don't think we've met."

"This is Hector Doink," Archie Neil said. "I mentioned him as one of our storytellers."

"Where did you get a name like 'Doink'?"

"It means 'Little Donald'—in Gaelic—only it's kind of slang," Archie Neil explained.

"My God, he's not very little," Brian said.

"Well," said Hector, "and Tommy Nancy MacLean doesn't wear skirts."

Father John Angus Rankin squeezed past them on his way for more tea. He said, "Ask Archie Neil what his name has in common with the Pope."

"Nothing as far as I'm concerned," Paddy said. And Brian Sutcliffe said, "I give up."

"It's the definite article," Archie Neil teased.

"Aww, bull," Paddy said.

"Well, it's true. In all of Scotland, there are only three who have the distinction of having the word 'the' in front—that's the Queen, the Pope, and the Chisholm."

"Don't forget the devil, eh?" Paddy added.

"Paddy," Archie Neil said, "I'll tell you a little story about Hector." Brian was torn, wanting to jump up and signal Ron Gillis to get the tape running, but not wanting to break the mood of the story. Afterward, he was sorry he didn't have it on tape.

"Hector Doink was a very active and athletic fellow. Look at him now, so you can just imagine what he was like when he was young. And he was telling me one time cruising for lumber—you remember, Hector?"

"Indeed I do. And a cold winter. Cold as today. I was cruising for lumber in the State of Maine."

"And he was admiring the trees," Archie Neil continued. "There was one particular tree he was looking at. He said that he looked up and he estimated that from the ground to where the first limbs were was at least forty-five feet. It was just a beautiful tree.

"And just when he was attentively looking at the tree, he heard some crashing behind him and there—not five feet from him—was one of those big brown bears, just beginning to rear up on its hind legs.

"I asked him, 'Hector, what did you do?'

"'What could I do?' he said. 'There was only that tree and the limbs up forty-five feet. But I took one spring into the air.'

"And I said, 'Did you make it, Hector?'

"'Not going up,'" he said. 'But I caught them on the way down.'"

Laughing, Brian stood up and got Ron Gillis's attention. For him, it was a combination of a good time and work. With difficulty, the room was quieted somewhat. Then he crouched down again with Hector and Archie Neil. Others were leaning in around them, making a little cave of expectant people. Weeks later, at another taping, Brian would lead Archie Neil back around to retell the story of Hector and the Bear.

"You're a strong man, Hector."

"You want to talk about strong men," said Hector Doink, "you want to talk about the Giant MacAskill. But did you ever see any of his people? I seen his sister in North River. She was a big woman. I went up at the house and I met a girl at the door. 'Where's MacAskill's sister?'

"'She's over there. You can go over and you'll see her.'

"I went over. And do you know what she was doing? She was making fence. She was knittin' a wire fence with two crowbars.'"

Archie Neil said to Brian, "You know, Hector was in the

war," his nasal tone exaggerating the vowels, imitating Hector. "And he met the Queen when he was in England."

"Hold it," Brian said. "Is this something that you should introduce on the tape?"

Into the microphone, Archie Neil started again: "The boys in the living room have passed the dipper and we've rounded up some tales, and a couple of ghost stories and excellent music. First, let's hear from Hector Doink MacDonald, who will tell us about his experience back in the days of the World War."

"Well, Archie Neil, I didn't register for the draft. No. I didn't think much of the army life or the war. Fact is, I didn't think about it at all until them two army fellahs found me working in the woods. They took me off right there. Had to leave everything, you know. The bucksaw, the axe, my lunch bucket on a stump. Went into the army all right. Served five years. Only good thing about it was I met the Queen."

"You wouldn't know the Queen if you did see her," said Paddy from across the room.

"Well, I ought to know. I was there. I was walking by Buckingham Palace one day. The Queen, she happened to look out the pantry window. She kinda knocked on it, you know, like this." Hector rapped his knuckles on the table. "And she made a sign for me to come in. I goes in and saw she was making biscuits. She wiped the flour off her hands and says, 'Hello, Hector. I'm glad you're over here fightin' for us. Come in and sit down for a tea. Listen, how is Donald Ranald Dan?'"

"Oh, now that's a lie," Paddy laughed. Others were laughing too.

"Those biscuits were some good," Hector said. "Never even my mother—or Margaret neither—could make better.

"But that's not all that happened with the war. Now, when I come back to Broad Cove, I was fearful lonesome for the woods. So I went to look for my bucksaw. The damn thing was there alright, but it was all rusted, hardly a tooth left. I threw it away. I think the beavers ate all the axe handle out. I looked on the stump, and there was my lunch can all rusted. I opened the can and looked inside, and the thermos was still in it. I opened the thermos and drank the tea. Upon my soul, it was still hot."

After the laughter, Archie Neil spoke into the mike: "I'll make a wager that when Hector Doink meets St. Peter at the Pearly Gates, the tea will still be hot in the thermos."

Brian stood up now and carefully worked his way to the far side of the room. Archie Neil would carry it from here.

"Now we'll hear a story from that master of detail in storytelling and folklore, Dan Angus Beaton from Blackstone. Dan's story, called 'The Red Thread,' comes from old beliefs that might have come to the Scots from contact with early Normans. It is a superstition that stays with some of our older people. A red thread, or yarn, has several groups of knots in it and each knot represents either a wish or a curse. The space between groups of knots is the time for the curse to take effect. Now let's hear the story from Dan Angus himself."

Dan Angus Beaton leaned toward the microphone. His delivery was precise and strong:

"To start, I have to tell you, Archie Neil, that this story is as true as I'm sitting here. I was twelve years old and my father was working on the railroad.

"In those days, the cart was the most useful implement on the farm. It had to be kept in shape. We had to take the cartwheels and have new hubs and spokes put in. One time we went to the forge and they told us to leave the work with them. They couldn't do it right away. They said to come the next day and they would have the wheels ready.

"So the next day, I brought my uncle's cart down for the wheels. My father came with me. When we got there, they had another hour's work to do on the wheels. The man doing the work said, 'Go into the house and the women will make you tea until we're through.' We did.

"There was this real old lady in her 90's, knitting with red yarn. She talked to my father in Gaelic. She came from Scotland as a young girl of seven years old. 'My, my,' she said. 'We had a terrible loss here this morning.'

"My father asked what she had lost.

"'We had a beautiful steer in the barn. When the men went out this morning, it was dead. It was to be our fall and winter's meat, and now we haven't any.'

"'What happened? Did he get hung up in his rope?'

202

"'Indeed, no. He never had a rope around his neck. He was in a box stall.'

"'He musta been sick then.'

"'It wasn't a sickness either.'

"'Well, it had to be something killed him.'

"'I know,' she said. 'But if I thought it was Black John that did this to us, I'd put this red thread to work and there wouldn't be an animal alive on his farm tomorrow.'

"'Those are pretty strong words. How would that be possible?'

"'Oh indeed, it would be possible,' the old lady said. 'Many is the time I put the red thread to work. Look into the matter yourself.

"'Just around a year ago, I put it to work. There was a fellow who had wheels—the same as you. From Inverness. The wheels wasn't ready and he came in for tea and he was awful cross and dirty about the wheels not being ready. One of our men was sick three or four days, that was why. After we had treated him good and royally with tea and biscuits, he hauled off and gave the dog an awful dirty kick as he was going out the door. Indeed, it made me so mad I put the red thread to work on him. The leg that kicked the dog certainly wouldn't kick him the next morning. It was darn well broke.'

"My father knew the man she was taking about and made a point of seeing him to get to the bottom of the red thread. He never said a word about the old lady, though.

"'I heard you had your leg broken,' he said to the fellow.

"'It was. I was away at the forge. When I got home, a big brown horse, a quiet animal, never raised a foot to kick in his life. But when I was hitching harness, he kicked me. Broke my leg so bad, Dr. MacMaster in Inverness sent me to Antigonish. Two months before I got home. The swelling was that bad.'

"Well, me and my father, we walked carefully around the dog when we went out their door after that. We had respect for the old lady's dog."

During a taping break, someone across the room was telling a joke—something about Alex and Sarah riding together to a picnic. He hit Sarah's bike accidentally and put her in the ditch.

The next day the story was all over that Alex, with a queer rig between his legs, was on top of Sarah in the ditch.

"Whoa, I hope that's not on tape," Brian said. "X-rated stuff. Archie Neil, how about that story you were telling Buddy awhile ago, the one about the Buick. That's a spooky one and I wondered if it was true."

"True as I'm sitting here," Archie Neil said with a grin directed at Dan Angus.

"But the thing is," Archie Neil said, more seriously, "this is fact and can be checked out any number of ways if you care to. This is what happened. In South West Margaree, there is a sharp turn about four miles from the Forks—people now call it Aucoin's Turn. People kept saying that there were strange lights there and—you know how it is these days—some people have to have scientific explanations. They said it was phosphorescent gas from the damp soil around the brook. Then one night, Sandy Aucoin was driving home from Inverness, and he had an accident—the car, a soft-top MacLachlan Buick, rolled into a ditch and he was killed.

"There's not much traffic on that road and it was several hours before he was found. It was the headlights that somebody noticed—otherwise, it might have been morning before it was discovered. Now that this happened the local people were saying that the lights they saw were a forerunner of poor Sandy's accident. But the thing was that for two years people were still seeing the same lights, and nobody liked going down that stretch of road after dark. Then Sandy's brother Charlie was on the same spot—when the exact same thing happened to him. He too was killed when his car rolled. His son who was with him, never quite recovered. That is why that curve is called Aucoin's Turn. After the second accident, the lights were never seen there again."

It stayed fairly quiet after that story was told. Archie Neil said into the mike, "We have a treat in store: Dan Angus and Kinnon Beaton on the fiddle, with Betty Lou on the piano, in a composition dedicated to the memory of Father John Allan Gillis. Following is a tune called 'Miss Drummond of Perth.' All our regular audience knows the music of this outstanding musical family."

The Beatons played and Margaret worked her way over to Archie Neil to find out if he wanted more tea. He said no, got her to empty his ashtray, and lit up another cigarette.

"Next we have another Broad Cove man. Paddy MacDonald—tell us a ghost story."

"Our parish priest, Father Stanley, didn't believe in ghosts, eh? He was not superstitious and all that and so when he moved into the Glebe House in Broad Cove, he didn't pay any attention to the stories about ghosts. He was replacing a priest who was supposed to come from Montreal by boat, but on the way to Cape Breton, the boat sank and he drowned. Father Stanley, he got help with the parishioners with settling in, but he didn't have a housekeeper, and he was pretty lonely. But he was not afraid. No attention to the ghost stories at all.

"But one night, he was uneasy and kept waking up. He turned over in bed and there was a person at the foot of his bed. It was hard to see it, maybe it was his imagination, so he put on his light. Yes, it was there. A man he didn't recognize at all. He was all wet, his clothes, eh?

"The man told him that he was the priest that was supposed to come to Broad Cove, but drowned. He said he had made promises when he decided to go to Cape Breton, and that Father Stanley now had to do them for him. One was to do something about the drinking in the parish. Two, he was to bring back unity among the neighbours, and Three—well, if he did the first two, he would come back and tell him Number Three. Then the ghost, or whatever it was, disappeared right there in front of his eyes. With the light on.

"Well, Father Stanley figured he'd better do what the ghost said, eh? So, the next day, he was walking around Inverness trying to figure it all out. He saw this chap weaving and stumbling down the street and figured this was as good a place to begin as any. He watched him go into a bar. Father Stanley had this idea how to go about getting this man to stop drinking, and he went and got a big earthworm. He went into the bar and sat down next to the drunk. He put the worm in the chap's whiskey and the worm died.

"'What do you think of that?' he asked the man.

"The man reached down, picked the worm out of the whiskey, and gulped down the drink. 'If you drink plenty of whisky,' the man told Father Stanley, 'you'll never have worms.'

"Father Stanley knew then that he had a lot of work to do on Number One."

Archie Neil moved into his introduction for the next story. When the final editing was done in the studio, he would probably add a short reply to Paddy MacDonald, but for now it was important to collect the stories and songs.

"I doubt if you'll get many clergymen to admit that they believe in ghosts," Archie Neil said. "But we all know that there are strange things that happen in the course of our lives, some of them are explainable, and some of them seem to have no natural explanation. Such is the case with this story by Father John Angus Rankin of Glendale. Father Rankin is familiar to most people in Cape Breton, and much beyond the Causeway too, for that matter. He was one of those behind the famous Glendale Fiddlers' Festival, and has led so many grand finales at concerts that he is said to have the best-known back in Nova Scotia. Not only that but he has a few stories of ghosts that open the mind to possibilities we may not have dreamed of before. He will share one of those stories with us now."

Father John Angus spoke so softly that the listeners had to be quiet, and the technical people adjusted their levels. His voice was smooth, a little roll to it, a little eerie as he told the story.

"This happened while I was Dean of Men at St. FX, and I never was able to explain the haunted room in the dorm in ordinary ways. There were just too many coincidences.

"I went with the football team to a game against Mount Allison in Truro. We ate at a restaurant, and when we came home from the game, there was a phone call for me. It was the woman who ran the restaurant, and she claimed that one of the boys had taken $500 from the counter in her restaurant. Money she needed to pay off bills.

"Well, I gathered the boys and confronted them with it. Oh, I really did hate to think one of them would do a thing like that. But none of them owned up to it, and you know, I have been working with people a long time, and it is hard to fool me. I really didn't think any of them stole the money. So it remained a mystery.

"That summer, one of the boys—we'll call him Danny—went to Western Ontario to work in the mines, and while he was there, he was killed. The next September, I put two freshmen in Danny's former room in the dorm. Within ten days, they came to me complaining about their room. They couldn't sleep in it. It wasn't something they saw or could hear—it was like there was someone in the room, something eerie, a feeling that there was a presence sliding along the wall, searching. I ignored them for awhile, but it was clear they were really upset, and they seemed level-headed enough in other ways. So I gave them another room and put two other boys in their room. Those new boys were there only a week or so, and they said the same thing. It was like there was something electrical—the hair on the back of their necks would bristle—there was something there.

"The room became vacant again and I got one of the janitors and we searched every inch of the room. It was just an ordinary dorm room with a closet in it. I slid my hand against the wall over a shelf, and discovered a small hole in the gyprock. I put my hand in the hole and found a vase—a cheap one—like you find in some restaurants where they might stick an artificial flower in it. It had a narrow neck. But I could see rolled up bills in it. Five hundred dollars exactly. I thought of the woman and called her, finding out first that, yes, she had stuffed the money in a vase. Maybe Danny had taken it as a souvenir without realizing that there was money in it.

"I often wondered if Danny only knew after he was dead—or if he knew before, and it was hanging on his conscience. It is something we will discover in the next life, not this one. But there was never a problem with the room after that money was returned."

Archie Neil spoke quietly into the mike to maintain the mood. "With that strange encounter with the unknown, let's now hear another from Jim St. Clair. Jim is a Harvard graduate, and now a teacher living in Mull River where his MacFarlane people came from. He spent a lot of his young years away from Cape Breton, but you can't take Cape Breton out of the boy. He's here today with a true story called 'Bòchdan Grieve,' straight from history."

Jim leaned in toward the mike, an elbow on the table. His

strong, rich voice hushed the listeners. He sounded as though he were speaking directly to just one person.

"If you go to Glencoe," he said, "and walk about 300 yards off from the road in one spot, there is a mound of stones in a grove of hemlocks. There lie the remains of Thomas Grieve, or as the local people call him, Bòchdan Grieve. About 1840, he was a poor stevedore in Glasgow, Scotland, working on the wharves. He was unfortunate enough to fall in love with the sister of one the merchants, and when he went to the merchant's office to announce his intention of marrying her, the merchant laughed in his face. 'You are too poor,' he said in an insulting way. So Grieve left, heartbroken, thinking to himself that he would give his soul to marry the merchant's sister.

"Well, he was determined, and for years worked hard. He earned a small fortune through wholesale trading, and went to the merchant's office again and asked. He brought money with him to show that he was no longer poor.

"Again, the merchant laughed in his face and told him he was not in her class. Enraged, Grieve struck the merchant who lurched backward, falling, hitting his head on the fender of a fireplace. He was dead.

"Grieve was terrified. He ran down the long hills to the shore, where a ship was just casting off lines to go to Halifax. He jumped from the wharf and went aboard, and as he looked back he saw the merchant's sister, the woman he loved and wanted to marry, standing at the door of the office, weeping. He could also see policemen running in his direction, with them an enormous black dog with fiery eyes.

"A sailor who saw him jump aboard ship came to talk to him. 'Mister, I don't know what you did. But I would advise that when we get to the first port, row away from the ship under cover of darkness. Find a place to live surrounded by water and go far inland. The devil will not be able to harm you there.'

"Grieve jumped ship at Ship Harbour, which we now call Port Hawkesbury. He went far inland, following Mull River, and settled himself in a lean-to not far from Glencoe. He bought the land shortly afterwards. The first night on his own land, he could see—coming over a rise of land—a black dog with fiery eyes, and it barked and snarled at him.

"He saw the dog off and on for years. It was always watching him as he went about his work, and he dreamed of it at night.

"In 1880 or '85, Thomas Grieve summoned neighbours—one of them was my great-grandfather—and told them he was going to die and to bury him immediately after death, covering the grave high with heavy stones from the chimney. As the watchers prepared him for burial, they saw the body shrinking, shrinking, until it was the size of a large doll. The men were frightened.

"They dug a hole and buried him under heavy chimney stones as he asked. When they were done, they saw a large black dog at the edge of a clearing. It turned, walked away. And many times after that, on a still night, the people of Mull River and Glencoe can hear the baying of this strange black dog. Sometimes, I can hear it myself from my back steps. That is the story of Bòchdan Grieve."

"Cut," Brian said, in the stilled room, everyone listening for the baying of the black dog. "God, that was a good one, Jim. Archie Neil, we need a lively tune to end—time's up for this show—a quick sign off. We'll take a break and begin another session."

Archie Neil took the mike. "Now that we've chilled you with ghosts, we'll warm you up again with one of my favourite recordings of John Allan Cameron, 'The Lord of the Dance.' But first, I want to mention the pair of shoes on the poster advertising this summer's Broad Cove Concert. There is a story with that.

"One frequent performer at Broad Cove was a man by the name of Don Riley, a comedian and dancer. His bronzed shoes are now in the Port Hastings museum. He was one of a kind, thin, raw-boned, and he had his own peculiar form of stepdancing. While dancing, he would take his handkerchief out of his pocket and polish his shoes. I played violin for him many a time and people liked him so well that they always asked, 'Did Donald come yet?' When Don came, the festivities began. He gave a lot of laughter to the world.

"So long for now. Tha mi an dochas gun soirbhich cuisean leibh, I hope that things go well for you. We'll be seeing you next week."

During the break, most of the visitors were on their feet, making their way outside for air or down the hall to the bathroom. Someone was playing a fiddle in the yard. The kitchen was full, and a late arrival, fiddler Jerry Holland, stayed behind to tease Archie Neil. He asked him how the radio show got started.

Archie Neil thought a long moment and said, very seriously, "You could say it began before I was born. A long time before."

"I didn't mean what were the Chisholms doing when the earth cooled down. I meant who found who. I heard Brian Sutcliffe first met you at Broad Cove Concert."

"Ah, recent history—sure. I was thinking of my mother's stories, and of Papa. And the home they made that welcomed songs and tunes and stories. But you mean when Brian was camping at MacLeod's and he heard me telling stories, doing the emcee thing at the Broad Cove concert."

"How long have you been doing Broad Cove?"

"Well, Father John Hugh MacEachern has one year over me, and he was emcee at the first one in 1956. I emceed every single year after that, with him, and I still do."

"You must be older than God."

"Well, yes. He was in one of my classes at Widow Lord's. His writing skills were bad. Never could tell what He meant by anything."

"Well, I heard you and Father John Hugh trade off a few insults." Kinnon Beaton said, joining them.

"We're the best of friends," said Archie Neil. "And terrible teasers. We both love to be insulted on stage—by each other, that is. There was one time when he came out on stage to the mike and said, 'I think it's about time we give Archie Neil a big hand,' and so everybody clapped. And I was sitting up there all puffed out. Then Father John Hugh put out what I thought was his hand for a shake. But it was a big wooden hand on a stick. I felt like two cents for a second or so. He sure put that one over on me. I've pulled a few tricks on him as well."

"Nice to be teased in front of eight thousand people."

"Maybe more these days. You look out from the stage and there's a sea of faces. Out near the woods, there's cars with license plates from every state and province. And there's always a flotilla of travel trailers navigating around for a good view of the stage. Not bad for a bunch of volunteer workers."

"Well, I think what's going on in the tuning room back of the stage is the real circus," Jerry Holland observed. "If the world only knew."

"I think my own greatest experience at any concert was at the first Glendale Festival. Fr. John Angus is sitting right here today and he'll tell you this is true. He doesn't like to say it, but he healed me. I'll tell you fellows now but please don't tell Brian Sutcliffe—it will kill poor Brian that he doesn't have this on tape. But it's a simple story.

"I had broken my leg again. In my own living room. I tried to stand up without my brace, and the leg broke. A bad break. And weeks and weeks and weeks went by, and the X-rays showed it wasn't healing. Far from healed. And of course it meant I was inactive. And miserable. Very unhappy.

"Fr. John Angus wanted me to be an emcee at that first Glendale Festival. I wanted to do it as well. It was such an important day—just a great big shout that Cape Breton fiddling was damn well not dead. That was the message, although we said it in a tasteful way—over 100 fiddlers on stage that day. A beautiful day. It made a beautiful recording.

"But there were three or four steps to climb up to the stage. It might as well have been a mountain. I was very uncomfortable, sitting there in my wheelchair beside Fr. John Angus. And he wasn't feeling very well himself. He was counting on me and glad that I had showed. And he urged me on. He put his hand on my leg, and he said, 'You'll be okay. You can do it.'

"So then the time came. Margaret was upset. She thought I'd fall. But using the crutches, I somehow got up those steps. And a day or two later, I went to the hospital—and the X-rays showed that the bone was completely healed."

The CBC technicians were herding people back to the living room, getting speakers for the next taping settled in around the table, checking the microphones and connections. There had been a commotion on the arrival of a new batch of visitors. Somehow, they wedged themselves in along the kitchen counter, laughing and talking.

211

"You know, it's funny," Archie Neil reflected after very little rest. "We hear a story like that one from Jim St. Clair, and it brings to mind another one, and then somebody else remembers a story because of that one. I think we could go on and on like that. There are a lot of stories that have never been recorded or written down over the years. There are a few my mother told me. I think some of them were quite old stories—"

"Wait, let's get this on tape," Brian suggested. "Keep that idea and use it for the next intro."

Word got around the house quickly—"They're taping!"— and the noise subsided, somewhat.

"Ceud mile failte. This is Archie Neil speaking. Recently I was talking to friends about some of the older stories that are still being told in Cape Breton. Many storytellers have passed away through the years, and as time takes its toll from each and every one of us, we may feel a sort of resentment against it for what it has done. What we do not realize, of course, is that in most cases time leaves something with us for everything it takes. It leaves memories, and memories are what these programs are all about.

"My mother was a MacFarlane of the Kintail MacFarlanes, and her stories had an influence on my own style of storytelling. I feel intensely that, because of her, I have a place in tradition. Not only the stories she told, but the love of stories, the storytellers she gathered around her, the many examples I heard and saw.

"But my mother herself—she was a great entertainer and sang Gaelic songs and she told me the stories behind the songs, some of them coming from old Scottish folklore. There is one that comes to mind, I can't remember the song exactly, but I remember the story, as my mother told it. I think the name of the song is 'I would take a drink from one who is dear to me.' The story goes like this.

"A young Scottish maiden became pregnant. The father of the child would not acknowledge her, and her noble family could not forgive her. Her life was made so bitter and unhappy by her enraged father, that she fled to a distant town where she was not known. There were not many choices for women in her predicament and taking an assumed name, she took service as a maid to make a living. For many years she remained in that household and no one knew her true identity.

"Now, the nobleman for whom she was working was staging a big celebration, and she was one of the maids serving the guests. At the dinner she recognized among the rich guests her own brother, but he did not recognize her, although he was struck by her beauty and grace.

"He broke protocol by offering her a drink, and later, because she had a good voice, she was asked to sing for the guests. She sang a song that she composed on the spot, and it began to register on her brother that he knew this young woman, and the words of her song confirmed it: he knew she was his sister. He knew her when she sang the song, 'I would take a drink from one who is dear to me.' He was happy, and in front of all the rich and noble people at the table he acknowledged her. And from then on, she was restored to her rightful place in her father's home."

Archie Neil paused. Then:

"Now, ladies and gentlemen, we will hear from a fiddler who is no longer with us, but whose music still lives and influences many of our best fiddlers today. The fiddler is my own brother, Angus Chisholm. Both Angus and I learned to fiddle from Johnny Stephen White from Margaree and on the same day we both learned to scratch out our first tune, 'Cock of the North.' At first, we didn't know a music note from a rabbit track, but we learned new tunes from hearing our sisters jig them for us. I can still hear my sister Willena jig us the verse of one song we really loved. It went: 'When I get married, won't I be good—I'll make my wife take in the wood, and make my tea in the morning.' We all loved music in our family, but Angus was the one true musician. We'll hear now two numbers from his early recordings: the first is a strathspey called 'The Dusty Miller,' and the second is 'The Old Time Wedding Reel.' After that, I'll share with you a story about my father, Archie Chisholm, and more stories and music from our friends here on 'Archie Neil's Cape Breton.'"

He lit another cigarette; the room was filled with Angus's wonderful fiddling. Archie Neil had both elbows on the table, the cigarette held in front of his face, his eyes closed.

"There were five Archie Chisholms around Margaree at about the same period of time: Big Archie and Archie Ban—these two were brothers—Archie Big William; Archie, who was young; and my father. So mail would not get mixed up, Papa was called Archie A. or 'Archie the Teacher.' The A had no significance in his name.

"My father was a teacher, and my mother was always at home. She was a big woman, close to six feet. She was very musical. She did not have any formal education, but was a great reader. My father had formal education, to high school, not university. He had a teacher's license.

"There was a mischievous smile behind a lot of what my father said and did. He could think of pranks, and far-fetched stories for the gullible.

"The house was full of people almost every night. Some were there so much that they became a nuisance.

"One boy, we'll call him Charlie, about nineteen, would be at the house at all times of the day or night, with my brother Donald, who was the same age. You couldn't eat, sleep, talk, or anything without Charlie being there. Charlie liked everything but praying—and he never wanted to get caught in a bind where he would have to say the rosary. He hated being on his knees for the length of a whole rosary.

"We had to say the rosary every night. At a certain hour, my father gathered us for the rosary, and you had to be very formal and quiet. Sometimes we fell asleep, sometimes we'd fire things at each other behind my father's back. We didn't mean to be irreverent or anything like that; it was just that we were too young and restless to be quiet that long. It was different praying with my mother, not so formal.

"Knowing that Charlie was averse to being caught so that he had to say the rosary, my father decided to spring a surprise. He grabbed the rosary off the hook, and said in a stern voice: 'We are going to say the rosary.' Charlie was intimidated and didn't dare leave at that awkward moment.

"Charlie put his cap on the floor and scrunched down on his knees, using his hat for a cushion. He was in very poor cheer. My father planned to prolong this as much as possible, and he decided to add The Way of the Cross to the usual rosary—

another twenty-five minutes. At the end of this, my father really opened up on the rosary—giving the Mysteries, and their meaning. We had never heard this rigmarole before! After the rosary, we recited a litany. When that was finished, he announced another decade of the rosary for the souls in Purgatory.

"This was too much for Charlie. He was inching away, trying to slide the cap out from under his knees, to make a break for it. My father announced another decade of the rosary for somebody by the name of Fidel Chiasson. We had never heard of him.

"Charlie was overcome. He had more of a bellyful of prayer than he could stand. He grabbed his cap, jumped up, and yelled: 'To Hell with him!' and ran out of the house and down the road as if the demons were after him. For a month Charlie never darkened our door."

And the afternoon went on and on.

Paddy MacDonald told the story of the Liberal who died and went to Heaven, and who left such a good record that St. Peter offered him the job of tending the Golden Gates. But he was nervous, wanted to know what to do in different cases— "'Lord save us,' he said, 'I can't take this job. What am I going to do when the Tories start coming through?'

"'Look boy,' St. Peter said, 'you don't have a worry in the world. I have been here two thousand years, and there wasn't any of them made it this far yet.'"

Dan Angus Beaton told the story of the Black Captain—his great-grandmother once rode with the captain on horseback— and the Black Captain later sold his soul to the devil—and how the devil not only took his soul but he even took the Black Captain's remains.

Father John Angus told about the time his own father returned from the dead, owing a debt—and of what Father John Angus went through to prove the truth of what he had seen.

And Alex John MacIsaac took the microphone to tell the sad, sad story of the fellow from Mabou Coal Mines who got an oversized herring in his net and kept it alive in a bucket—kept it as a pet. And used to take it out of the water and play with it, and then put it back. Kept it out longer and longer. Till finally that herring could breathe air. Got along fine out of water.

215

"He used to follow him around to the barn," said Alex John, "and here and there. And this certain day, the old fellow was goin' after the cows, and the herring was coming right behind him. And they were going across the bridge, over the brook. And didn't the herring fall off into the brook—and the poor thing drowned."

And in between, Jerry Holland and Buddy MacMaster took turns playing the fiddle. A beautiful afternoon.

Archie Neil ended that day's taping with the story about the clergyman whose neighbour, Sandy, was continually drinking. "The priest was after him all the time to try and go a little bit sober, but nothing seemed to do any good—and Sandy still kept drinking. But on this particular occasion the priest met him, and he was very, very drunk. After having a long talk with him, Sandy said, 'Well, if I could only get about five dollars, that I could straighten up. I'll promise you, Father, that I won't drink any more.'

"The priest had quite a sense of humour—along with a sense of mercy and justice. He figured, Well, I'll just try him. He said, 'You pray. You pray to the Virgin Mother, and you just might get the five dollars.'

"And at the same time, the priest put his hand in his own pocket. All he had was three dollars, but he slipped the three dollars into Sandy's coat pocket without him knowing it at all.

"Okay. About two or three hours later. And of course the fellow did possibly what I would have done myself. He headed for the nearest grog shop and added to his jag.

"But he met the priest again later—and this time he was really loaded. And the priest said, 'Sandy, this is an awful shame.' And Sandy was at the point where he didn't know to whom he was speaking or anything else. And he said, 'Look, who are you anyway, talking to me like that?'

"The priest answered, 'You don't know me. Look, Sandy, I could be your Saviour.'

"'Well, then you're just the man I want to meet,' said Sandy. 'Listen. Tell your mother she still owes me two dollars.'"

Later that night, the technicians and the producer and all the equipment were gone. Margaret and Archie Neil watched the last of the visitors drive away, and although the night was cool they stayed out awhile, looking across the Margaree River, watching it disappear into the dark. Just a single light bulb from the porch, and the passing of an occasional car. He had no idea what Margaret was thinking. He knew she was there, she was steady, she loved him. Silent, he talked to himself: I have what I never thought I'd have, and I am grateful for what I have. A home, a family. And then, like a little poem, he thought: A wife. A life.

He said nothing aloud to Margaret. She leaned down and kissed him on the top of his head.

"What did I do to earn that, Margaret?"

"Nothing," she said, backing the wheelchair and turning it and pushing a smiling Archie Neil up the ramp and into the house.

Some Awards and Achievements of Archie Neil Chisholm

1926—Archie Neil began a teaching career at South River Lake School that was to span 64 years as a public schoolteacher and principal, and as a teacher for Continuing Education and GED classes.

1936—Graduated from Nova Scotia Teachers' College, Truro.

1950—Conquered alcoholism at age 43. Became a frequent speaker at Alcoholics Anonymous meetings at Talbot House, and other places.

1956—Conservative candidate in the Inverness County election for Members of the Legislative Assembly. Second candidacy in 1960. In 1986, he was given an award of recognition from the Progressive Conservative Party of Cape Breton Highlands-Canso for "dedication and diligent work."

1956—Began fund raising for the Canadian National Institute for the Blind, and for the March of Dimes. Similar volunteer work continues to the present, including the Ability Fund, the Red Cross, Children's Aid Society of Nova Scotia, Canadian Paraplegic Association, Christmas Daddies, and others.

1957—Archie Neil's first appearance as emcee for the Broad Cove Concert; he is still emceeing this event. In 1981, organizers of the 25th Broad Cove Concert presented Archie Neil with an "outstanding Scot" award. He has emceed hundreds of concerts, festivals, and fund-raising events in dozens of locations, like the Gaelic Mod at St. Ann's and Highland Village Day at Iona.

1967—Archie Neil graduated with a Bachelor of Arts degree from St. Francis Xavier University, at age 59 the oldest member of the class, which earned him an article in *Time* magazine. Fellow graduates presented an award for "outstanding ability, devotion and effort as a persevering scholar of the Class of 1967."

1972—A founding member of the Glendale Fiddlers' Association, Archie Neil helped emcee the first Glendale Festival of Scottish Fiddling in 1973, which was organized to disprove the idea of "the vanishing Cape Breton fiddler." In 1986, he received an award of recognition during the 25th Glendale Ceilidh.

1977—Inverness District Schools award for his support of Model Parliaments. Awarded again in 1978 and 1983.

1979—Hosted "Archie Neil's Cape Breton" on CBI/CBC, a series of half-hour radio programs first broadcast in the Maritimes in January. The program was aired nationally in 1982. "Archie Neil's Cape Breton" included conversation, music, songs, and stories from Cape Breton. He is still frequently interviewed and featured on radio.

1979—Recognition from the Cape Breton Fiddlers' Association for many years of "outstanding service, dedication and continued support of Cape Breton Style Violin Music." He was a founding member of the Fiddlers' Association. In 1989, the Fiddlers' Association hosted a testimonial banquet in honour of Archie Neil Chisholm in Baddeck. Judge Hugh MacPherson spoke of him as "an outstanding educator, Gaelic speaker, storyteller, and promoter of Scottish ceilidhs."

1980—Consultant and contributor to *Songs of the Valley*, a collection of the poetry of Walter Scott MacFarlane, edited by Kay MacDonald and Pat MacFarlane.

1980—Award from the Margaree Summer Festival for "continued dedication to the success of the Festival." The same organization gave Archie Neil a special recognition for being Grand Marshall in 1988.

1981—Consultant and contributor to the publication *The Cape Breton Fiddler*, edited by Allister MacGillivray.

1981—Award of Appreciation from Recreation Inverness County for "outstanding contribution of volunteer efforts towards making our community a better place to live."

1983—Recognition from the Canadian Rehabilitation Council for the Disabled for "outstanding achievement in overcoming a physical handicap."

1984—Began conducting classes for the International Elderhostel Program, with sessions at the Normaway Inn and the Gaelic College. He has conducted 39 classes to date.

1985—Host and narrator of "Land and Sea's" Christmas special for CBC television. Filmed at his home in November, the Chisholm house was thoroughly decorated for Christmas inside and out. The special featured Cape Breton music and storytelling. He narrated and/or appeared in several films, including "The Blood is Strong," "Heritage Remembered," and tourism productions such as "The Ceilidh and Fleur-de-Lis Trails."

1985—"Cash for Kids" crusade through CIGO radio, raising funds for the Children's Aid Society of Nova Scotia. Archie Neil is still involved in this project.

1986—Appreciation for "an important contribution" to the Canadian Pavilion during the World Exposition in Vancouver as a storyteller and discussion leader on Cape Breton folklore. Participated in two radio broadcasts from Expo '86 grounds.

1986—During Rick Hansen's "Man in Motion" round-the-world tour, Archie Neil was instrumental in raising over $16,000 through radio stations CJFX and CIGO. Archie Neil presented the funds to Hansen in Port Hawkesbury.

1986—Award of appreciation from Canadian Paraplegic Association "in grateful recognition of tireless and outstanding service in pioneering the 1985 fund-raising campaign in Cape Breton."

1986—Interviewed for Issue 42, *Cape Breton's Magazine*. A portion of this interview is in the book *Cape Breton Lives*, published in 1988.

1987—Recognition from the Canadian National Institute for the Blind "in appreciation of untiring and dedicated volunteer service to blind and visually impaired people." Awarded to Archie Neil again in 1989 and 1990.

1988—A volunteer for the CTV "Christmas Daddies" television campaign. Is still involved in this work.

1989—Appreciation award, as an honorary member, from Lions International on Charter Night at Whycocomagh and Area Lions Club. In 1991, he was recognized by the Whycocomagh and Area Lions Club for "outstanding service."

1989—Appreciation by the Margaree Kinsmen on the 10th anniversary of Archie Neil's honorary membership. He is also an honorary member of the Margaree Forks Fire Department.

1989—Appreciation from the Inverness District School Board and the Inverness County Recreation/ Tourism Department "for continuous contributions to adult education and GED in Inverness County." In 1991, he was honoured by former GED students and presented with a portrait of himself by artist Peter Rankin.

1990—Recognition from the Inverness County Heritage and Advisory Committee on the occasion of his 83rd birthday.

1991—Award of Merit from the Nova Scotia Highland Village Society: "To Margaret and Archie Neil Chisholm, two special people who have travelled miles and shared knowledge to maintain Cape Breton Scottish culture."

Archie Neil serves on the following Advisory Boards: Nova Scotia Pensions, Canadian National Institute for the Blind, The March of Dimes, The Ability Fund, Inverness Hospital Ethics Committee, Canso Regional Vocational School, Canadian Consultative Commission on Multiculturalism.